F. E. Bentley
Pemerton
October 1962

THE DUCHESS OF MALFI

Sources, Themes, Characters

GUNNAR BOKLUND

HARVARD UNIVERSITY PRESS
CAMBRIDGE, MASSACHUSETTS · 1962

Distributed in Great Britain by Oxford University Press, London

Publication of this book has been aided by a grant from the Ford Foundation

Library of Congress Catalog Card Number 62–19212

Printed in the United States of America

Book Design by David Ford

TO HENRY HATFIELD

PREFACE

This book was originally planned as a companion volume to *The Sources of* The White Devil (1957), and some readers may still choose so to regard it. The purpose remains the same; to establish what sources Webster used, what his play is about, and how good a play it is. The difference is largely one of emphasis. Since the sources of *The Duchess of Malfi* are more easily surveyed than those of *The White Devil,* less space has this time been devoted to sources than to the tragedy itself, with a consideration of Webster's dramatic art in both plays as a natural conclusion.

It is impossible to state exactly how the advice of scholars and friends have influenced my work beyond what is duly indicated in the end notes. Long discussions of problems of research may lead to nothing, whereas casual observations on brief passages in the text may give rise to reflections of unexpected consequence. There are, however, more tangible debts of gratitude to pay. Professor H. W. Donner of Uppsala University has been a tower of strength to me at every stage of my work, as has Professor Kenneth B. Murdock of Harvard. By repeated grants-in-aid Uppsala University has facilitated my research, and by awarding me a Folger fellowship the Trustees of Amherst College and the Director of the Folger Shakespeare Library have made it possible for me to work for several months in a most congenial atmosphere. It is finally a pleasure to note that the courtesy and

efficiency of the staff of Harvard University Press have relieved
the author and his wife of many tasks to which they had been
looking forward with some dread.

G. B.

I Tatti, Florence
June 1962

CONTENTS

THE DUCHESS
OF MALFI

Sources, Themes, Characters

I ❦ The Story of the Duchess of Amalfi

The Historical Facts

The treaty of Granada in November 1500 virtually sealed the fate of the Kingdom of Naples. When the Franco-Spanish attack came in the summer of 1501, a few weeks of war were sufficient to force King Federico to capitulate. In September he left Ischia, his last place of refuge, to accept the offer of Louis XII to live in comfortable exile in France, and on November 9, 1504, the last Aragonian King of Naples died. His son Ferdinand, who had held out in Taranto against the forces of Gonsalvo de Cordoba until March 1502, spent the rest of his life in a Spanish monastery. Little more than a year later Gonsalvo ousted the French from Neapolitan territory and brought Naples under the Spanish crown. The Great Captain himself ruled the country as viceroy until 1508, when he was relieved by the Duke of Cardona.[1]

The disaster that had overtaken the royal line did not, so far as we can judge, seriously affect the fortunes of the children of Enrico d'Aragona, King Federico's half brother. Lodovico d'Aragona, Cardinal of Santa Maria in Cosmedin, remained an influential personage in Naples under the Spanish rule. Born in 1474, he had early shown remarkable prowess in the tilt, had been made a cardinal by Alexander VI, probably in 1494, and had, in spite of his holy office, fought the invading French in 1496.[2] Apart from two important diplomatic missions he spent his life in Naples and Rome. To judge from contemporary reports, he took his office as cardinal very seriously, had the best reputation, and enjoyed the particular favor of Julius II, whom he accompanied on the strenuous Bologna campaign in the winter of 1510–11. Now, as fifteen years earlier, the Cardinal of Aragon, dressed in steel, took command of soldiers. He was at the pope's side when Julius, also in armor, inspected his troops at the famous siege of Mirandola, and his descent made people consider him to be the candidate for the throne of Naples for whom, it was rumored, the pope was now looking.[3] This plan of Julius', if it was ever seriously entertained, came to nought with his death, but Lodovico d'Aragona still remained a man of considerable influence under Leo X. His newly erected Roman residence was what is now known as the Palazzo dei Penitenzieri, where his interest in art and music was much in evidence. But he was not only an impressive dignitary and a fastidious connoisseur; according to one of the great authorities on the age he was also "perhaps the best of the young cardinals." [4] Lodovico d'Aragona died in Rome in 1519 and was buried in Santa Maria sopra Minerva, where an inscription in his honor can still be seen.[5]

Carlo, the younger son of Enrico d'Aragona, took over the title of Marquis of Gerace from his brother when the latter was made cardinal, and ended his days without—as far as I have been able to ascertain—leaving any significant trace in historical documents. Considerably more, however, can be learned about his sister Giovanna.[6] In 1490, when she was no more than twelve years old, she was married to Alfonso Piccolomini who became Duke of Amalfi in 1493, and in 1498 she was widowed. Her son Alfonso was born early in the following year, and she was to have governed the duchy for him until he came of age. She did so for more than ten years, but in November 1510 she suddenly left Amalfi with the alleged intention of undertaking a pilgrimage to Loreto. It was soon realized that this was only a pretext for escaping from Amalfi, for from Loreto she proceeded to Ancona, where she joined Antonio Bologna, formerly master of her household, whom she had secretly married. The couple did not long enjoy life and liberty. In October 1513 Antonio was killed in Milan, and Giovanna was probably murdered at Amalfi several months earlier. One of their children, a boy who cannot have been more than seven when his father died, escaped death, but his younger brother and sister were evidently murdered with their mother.[7] Their half brother Alfonso Piccolomini ruled as Duke of Amalfi until his death in 1559.

There is almost nothing in contemporary chronicles and diaries to connect Cardinal Lodovico and his brother with these events. In 1508 the duchess visited her brothers in Naples, and as late as August 1509 they made a pilgrimage to Amalfi and were magnificently entertained by her. No intimations that they suspected what was going on can be discovered in the records of these visits. The marriage of the duchess and the births of her first two children seem to have been kept effectively secret. But she evidently knew where her greatest danger lay, for she made her escape to Ancona at a time when the cardinal was fighting the enemies of the pope near Bologna and thus hardly in a position to take immediate action against an erring sister one hundred and fifty miles away.[8]

This is virtually all that can be learned from the historical documents in the case. For further information a source must be used that should obviously be treated with great caution: Bandello's *Il signor Antonio Bologna sposa la duchessa d'Amalfi, e tutti due sono ammazzati,* the twenty-sixth novella in part one of his collection.[9] A few additional details may be gathered from later accounts, almost exclusively among the so-called Corona manuscripts at Naples. Their independent value is, however, so slight that for all practical purposes Bandello's narrative is our only source of knowledge for most of the duchess' story.[10]

Fortunately Bandello was in a position to make a good novella of his material without deviating drastically from the historical facts. He probably knew Antonio personally; he may have been present at his murder and certainly heard the story of his life from one who was well acquainted with him.[11] It is true that part of the novella is based on hearsay only and that Bandello himself added both dialogue and much colorful detail, but where the outlines of his plot can be checked against established facts, they are almost invariably found to be correct. He also refers to a sufficient number of historical figures and events to make it possible to date the various incidents of the story with considerable, though far from perfect, accuracy.

It is thus clear that Antonio, who had served as master of King Federico's household in France, did not return to Naples until early in 1505, a fact which sets the date before which the secret marriage cannot have taken place. The details given by Bandello of the adventures of the lovers after their flight from Amalfi also help to establish a fairly reliable chronology. They were expelled from Ancona six or seven months after their arrival, i.e., in the summer of 1511, escaped to Siena, but met with the same fate there. When at last they tried to reach Venetian territory they were overtaken at Forlì; the duchess was seized and brought back to Amalfi with two of the children, while Antonio and his eldest son sought refuge in Milan.

As the war of the Holy League was raging in Romagna, Bologna, and Lombardy from January to June 1512—the battle of Ravenna was fought on April 11—it is improbable that the attempt to escape to Venice was made before the late spring of that year. As the French abandoned the city of Milan in June, Massimiliano Sforza was made Duke of Milan in August, and Bandello mentions that Antonio attached himself to Silvio Savelli, commander of Sforza's troops that besieged the still French-held castle, the time for the parting of the lovers and Antonio's arrival in Milan would be between June and, probably, September 1512. This fits in with Bandello's statement that Antonio lived in Milan for more than a year before he was killed; his death definitely occurred in October 1513.[12] There is unfortunately no way of finding out whether the duchess was really murdered with her little children and the chambermaid, nor can it be determined exactly where and how she met her death.

It should be obvious from this reconstruction of history that much of what happened still remains obscure. The possibility that an English dramatist, writing a century after the events, should have had extensive knowledge of the actual facts, must be regarded as remote.[13] The removal from this world of Antonio Bologna and his duchess was evidently neatly and expertly carried out. In comparison with the stir caused seventy-five years later by the murder of Vittoria Accoramboni, the discretion with which both revengers and victims behaved is remarkable. There was no scandal and little comment. If Bandello had not written his novella, Carlo d'Aragona, Giovanna Piccolomini and Antonio Bologna would have been no more than names in the history of a very minor duchy. Records would have told of family ties, mutual visits, rumors of a secret marriage, the flight to Ancona. That would have been all. But Cardinal Lodovico would not have remained obscure: whether he was the best of the young cardinals or not, he occupies a place in the history of the age in his own right.

Bandello

Although Bandello's novella has considerable value as a historical document, it is above all interesting as the first literary account of the life of the Duchess of Amalfi, the origin of several versions to follow. It is generally agreed that Webster did not use the Italian original as the *main* source of his play, but the possibility remains that he had access to it and changed and modified his plot and characters according to intimations in Bandello. It is definitely one of the probable sources of *The Duchess of Malfi*, and the extent to which it differs from later translations and adaptions should be established.

Bandello tells his story with commendable conciseness and lucidity. After having introduced his hero and heroine to the reader and clarified their situation, he brings them together and makes the Duchess, who is never mentioned by name, propose to Antonio. He accepts her and promises always to remain her humble servant; a chambermaid "to whom she had already confided her thoughts" is sent for, and the lovers declare themselves man and wife with her as their only witness.[14] As the reason for this secrecy is adduced the fear of the Duchess for the wrath of her brothers. The birth of their first child passes unnoticed, but when the second is born, rumors reach the ears of the brothers. To find out who is the father of the child they send spies to Amalfi, and Antonio soon begins to feel ill at ease. Suspecting the chambermaid of double-dealing and fearing the revenge of the Aragonian brothers, one of whom has particularly violent habits ("sa menar le mani"), Antonio suggests to his wife that he should go to Ancona together with the children, there to weather the storm which he expects will soon break.[15] He does not consider his wife's life in danger. The Duchess, who is now pregnant again, cannot long remain alone and, after a detour to the shrine of Loreto, joins her husband in his new home. She now reveals her secret to her servants, most of whom immediately leave her for fear of the consequences of her indiscretion. They do not forget to dispatch a messenger to Rome to inform the Cardinal and his brother of what has happened. The family life of the lovers at Ancona, where their third child is born, lasts for a few months, whereupon renewed flight and final capture follow as described before.

The details of the capture are of considerable interest. By the time the fugitives discover their pursuers, they are depicted as more dead than alive, which does not, however, prevent them from trying to escape as best they can. The Duchess soon sees that she and the two youngest children cannot get away and exhorts her husband to save himself, assuring him that her brothers have no evil designs against her. After accepting a purse with a large sum of money Antonio departs, shedding "infinite tears," and accompanied by his eldest son and four servants. The leader of the pursuing horsemen protests to the Duchess that no harm is intended against her, suggests that Antonio must have been tired of her thus to leave her without cause, and accompanies her to Amalfi, where she is supposed to resume her duties as guardian of the Duke, her son. Here she is strangled together with the children and the faithful chambermaid.

This is kept secret from Antonio, who remains inactive in Milan while his property in Naples is confiscated and agents are sent out with orders to kill him. When "il nostro Delio," probably Bandello himself, tries to warn him of the risks he is running, telling him that he knows for certain that the Duchess is dead, Antonio informs him that he has letters in which he is promised the return of his goods and a reconciliation with "monsignor illustrissimo e reverendissimo mio signore."[16] Soon afterwards Delio sees Antonio murdered in front of the church of San Francesco. The murderers, who all escape, are three men led by Daniele da Bozolo, a Lombard captain in the service of the Aragonian brothers.

Many names are mentioned in Bandello's story, but few characters emerge. Silvio Savelli is a soldier and Antonio's protector, Bozolo an officer in charge of a murder operation, Delio a decent and well-meaning gentleman. The Aragonian brothers are proud of their birth, ferocious of nature, and relentless in revenge, the Cardinal being definitely the leading spirit. The anonymous chambermaid, having been brought up by the Duchess, knows in advance of her plans to marry and is the only witness to the ceremony. She is suspected of treachery by Antonio; she accompanies her mistress on her perambulations, and is taken prisoner and strangled with her.

Considerably more is told about the Duchess and Antonio, the only persons to whose motives and thoughts Bandello pays any real attention. Antonio's virtues are repeatedly dwelt upon: he is "nobile, virtuoso ed onestamente ricco," an accomplished lute player, an excellent horseman and valiant in the field, also "bellissimo uomo, grande e ben formato." [17] His marriage is motivated by love, not by ambition, and his devotion to wife and children is beyond doubt. No criticism is leveled against this exemplary gentleman, unless Delio's shrug of the shoulders at his unrealistic faith in the good will of the Aragonian brothers should be taken as such.

On other occasions, however, Antonio's behavior is far from impractical. He suspects the chambermaid, he suggests his own flight to Ancona, he leaves his wife and children at Forlì in order to save himself. It may even be argued that he makes himself absolutely sure of the Duchess' love before he decides to engage his own feelings. If we analyze everything that Antonio says and does as a revelation of his character, we shall detect a streak of hesitancy and circumspection, perhaps also of selfish deliberation. But it seems highly improbable that Bandello wished to hint at such an interpretation. After the introductory note of eulogy, intended to explain and excuse the Duchess' choice, he treats Antonio in his most matter-of-fact manner. He is not expected to behave as a hero but as a prudent gentleman—an ideal of considerable force in Renaissance Italy. The reasons given by Antonio for his behavior, then, should be accepted as genuine: he tries to do his best not only for himself but also for his family. Once this point of view has been adopted, Antonio's conduct becomes considerably less reprehensible than it appears at first glance.

The case of the Duchess is presented with the same disillusioned attitude to human nature. "Di poca età, gagliarda e bella," believing that the taking of a competent lover is the natural solution to her problem, she decides that Antonio is the one best qualified for the office, whereupon she falls violently in love with him.[18] On second thought, however, she has religious scruples about unmarried love and prefers a secret betrothal. This is arranged with remarkable speed and capability, no indication whatever being given of the undesirability of such proceedings from the social and religious points of view. After the marriage she is completely passion's slave. Hers is certainly a love match, but Bandello has no illusions about the origin of her love: she wants to "goder la sua gioventù."[19]

There is an intimation of banter in her underhand way of proposing to Antonio, some dignity in the speech with which she disposes of her servants at Ancona, and considerable pathos in her resigned acceptance of captivity and death. But very little is made of this. Her death is mentioned, her suffering is not. It is her husband's danger that haunts her mind, not her own. Bandello's Duchess is primarily, indeed almost exclusively, a woman in love. In spite of the author's tolerant understanding of her situation she is never transformed into a martyr. Nor are the Cardinal and his brother regarded as inhuman monsters. What happened was all part of life, a cause for pity and perhaps for indignation, but hardly for astonishment or alarm.

The Corona Manuscripts

Considering the importance of the persons involved and the sensational nature of the main events, it is not surprising that manuscript accounts of the Duchess' life should have been written and preserved to modern times. The Biblioteca Nazionale in Naples has the lion's share of them; they are usually grouped together with equally sensational stories under titles such as *Successi tragici et amorosi* or *Avvenimenti lussuriosi e tragici*. These are, however, properly speaking, subtitles only. When the collection was first put together by the brothers Silvio and Ascanio Corona in the middle of the sixteenth century, they used the very appropriate name of *La verità svelata* for it. Their work was then copied and augmented by later writers, until the result was the present manuscripts, most of them dating from the early eighteenth century.[20]

The character of these accounts of the Duchess' life is disappointing in comparison with the richness and variety of the extant Vittoria Accoramboni material. With only one exception the Neapolitan documents are virtually identical with each other and show such a striking verbal similarity to Bandello's novella that there can be no doubt about their source. The manuscripts are thus relegated to the status of copies, of no value to the investigator unless they differ from Bandello on points where the use of independent information can be suspected.

The deviations from the original story are very few. All is consistently told from a Neapolitan point of view, with the result that the names of the persons with whom Antonio associated in Milan are misunderstood and distorted. But this shortcoming is compensated by the additional information given about more important characters, obviously thanks to better knowledge of local history. The Cardinal is identified as Don Luigi, his brother as Carlo, Marquis of Gerace, and their sister as Giovanna, married to Alfonso Piccolomini, Duke of Amalfi. Even the names of their parents and grandparents are provided. Where Bandello discreetly writes "voi . . . sapete come *un di loro* sa menar le mani," the manuscript account boldly substitutes *il Cardinale*.[21] Where Bandello allows the Duchess' chambermaid to remain anonymous, the manuscripts offer a choice of two names, Lucina Bonito and Beatrice Macedonio, Beatrice being the name of a maid of honor mentioned by Bandello with whom the chambermaid now seems confused. It should finally be observed that Antonio's surviving son, called Federico "in memory of the unfortunate King," according to the Coronas soon joins his father's relatives in Naples, where he is presumably allowed to complete his life in peace and obscurity.

There is, however, one version among the Corona manuscripts

that is obviously independent of Bandello and tells a slightly different story. It is part of the *Vita della principessa di Francavilla,* written by Filonico Alicarnasso, and it is quite brief.[22] The only characters mentioned are the Cardinal, Antonio, the Duchess, and their children. It is when she is invited to visit her brother in Rome that she decides to escape from Amalfi under the pretext of a pilgrimage, and it is when she arrives at Ancona that she is taken prisoner by the Cardinal's men. In this city the unfortunate Duchess is poisoned, the innocent children murdered, and "finalmente ucciso Antonio infelice e superbo." [23] As can be gathered from this, the author is hardly sympathetic towards the lovers; theirs is in his words an "istoria triviale e comune a tutti."

Belleforest–Painter

"Istoria triviale e comune a tutti." Although this disillusioned attitude to crime and violence is characteristic also of Bandello, it is not perpetuated by his French and English translators. To all intents and purposes Belleforest and Painter constitute one version, the few changes made by the Englishman being usually insignificant.[24] It should perhaps be noted that Antonio's murderer is condemned with more vigor in Painter than in Belleforest, and that the reaction of the Aragonian brothers to their sister's marriage, vehement already in French, is even more so in the English version. On the whole, however, Painter does no more than translate his text as best he can.

Belleforest, on the other hand, had no intention of translating literally. Although the incidents he describes are the same as in Bandello, his story is four times as long. Almost half of it is made up of direct speech: his characters are extremely fond of lecturing, both to themselves and to each other. Such profusion of dialogue and soliloquy might obviously be of great interest to a dramatist, but Belleforest's speeches and comments are seldom suggestive. The allusions to classical history, conspicuously lacking in Bandello, refer to the stock examples of vice and crime—

Nero, Caligula, Messalina, Semiramis—figures that have been used to point a moral since the days of Boccaccio and Chaucer. For Belleforest's main object is to point a moral; when he holds forth on his favorite topics of lust and cruelty, the ample material provided by Bandello does not suffice. His work is in fact a sermon rather than a "nouel"; his art is far removed from the detached storytelling of the Italian *novellieri*. But it should be noticed that this preacher castigates sin and vice wherever he finds it and that his attitude to the characters changes as the theme of his sermon demands: he heartily and vociferously condemns both the marriage of the Duchess and the vengeance of her brothers. Although he has struck commentators as intolerably priggish, his work has a wider range than appears at first sight.

Belleforest changes only minor details in the plot of his original. F. L. Lucas lists the following deviations:

(1) It is the waiting-maid who suggests the pilgrimage to Loretto. . .

(2) Belleforest definitely calls the story a *"tragédie"*; of the marriage he remarks *"voici le premier acte de cette tragédie";* Antonio's departure to Ancona completes the second act, his death the last.

(3) He changes Bandello's "Petrucci" to "Castruccio". . .

(4) Strangling is definitely mentioned as the manner of the Duchess's murder.[25]

To this should only be added that Belleforest does more than mention the strangling of the Duchess—Bandello does that too—he describes it at length, providing his readers with a detailed record of the words and deeds of both murderers and victims. This is, however, the only time when his predilection for dialogue and soliloquy leads Belleforest into adding to the plot of his original. The characters, on the other hand, are constantly tampered with, and here Belleforest makes his most significant contribution to the development of the Duchess' story. Some of the names in Bandello are augmented into crude character sketches, extremely heavy-handed, as an unimaginative moralist's interpretations of men's souls are apt to be, but provocative enough if tolerantly studied. Belleforest and Painter wrote in the conviction that their work would be seriously considered by benevolent readers. Let us grant them that privilege, which was after all readily granted by their contemporaries.

We should thus see in Belleforest's Delio something more than Bandello's courteous and passive gentleman. He is also "one very well learned, and of trim inuention, who very excellently hath endited in the Italian vulgar tongue." [26] Bozola is not only a Lombard captain who murders Antonio according to instructions received. He is now "inueigled with Couetousnesse, and hired for ready Money" and is condemned as "this bloudy beaste" and "Thys newe Iudas and pestilent manqueller." [27] The author is taking sides and wants his readers to do the same.

The chambermaid remains anonymous, but considerable attention is bestowed on her. She is "gentle and of a good mind and stomake, and loued hir mistresse very derely." [28] Her participation in the plot is the same as in Bandello, with the exception that she is the one who suggests the pilgrimage to Loreto. Her death, mentioned only in passing in the Italian novella, is now made much of:

The mayden seeing the pitious Tragedy commensed vpon hir maystresse, cried out a maine, cursing the cruell malice of those tormenters, and besought God to be witnesse of the same, and crying out vpon his diuine Maiesty, she humbly praied vnto him to bend hys iudgement agaynst them which causelesse (being no Magistrates,) had killed so innocent creatures. "Reason it is" (sayd one of the Tyrants) "that thou be partaker of thy maystresse innocency, sith thou hast bene so faythfull a Minister, and messenger of hir fleshly follies." And sodaynly caught hir by the hayre of the head, and in steade of a Carcanet placed a roape about her necke. "How nowe" (quoth shee,) "is this the promised fayth you made vnto my Lady?" [29]

The Aragonian brothers are at first treated as a unit with no more effort at differentiation than in Bandello. But when the message from Ancona arrives, their different characters emerge. Against the Duke, "transported with choler, and driuen into deadly furie," is set the Cardinal, "grinding his teeth togither, chattering forth of his Spanish mosel Jack an Apes Paternoster." [30] Although Belleforest makes both brothers share the responsibility for the murders, he cannot refrain from drawing particular attention to the strange activities in which the Cardinal is engaged. "But what? it was in the tyme of Iulius the second, who was more martiall than Christian, and loued better to shed bloud than giue blessing to the people." [31] No particular mention, however, is made of the warlike disposition of the Cardinal, nor is he ever referred to by his proper name.

His brother also remains anonymous and would, but for one passage, have to be written off as the same ill-defined revenger as in Bandello. But his spectacular outburst of fury at the reception of the unpleasant news from Ancona is an addition by Belleforest, one of the most remarkable he made to the story:

but this incarnate diuelish beaste the Woman, no force can subdue hir, no swiftnesse can approch hir mobility, no good mind is able to preuent hir sleightes and deceites, they seem to be procreated and borne againste all order of Nature, and to liue withoute Lawe, whych gouerneth al other things indued with some reason and understanding . . . Ah, false and vile bytch, I sweare by the Almighty God and by his blessed wounds, that if I can catch thee, and that wicked knaue thy chosen mate, I wil pype ye both sutch a wofull galiard, as in your imbracements ye neuer felt like ioy and mirthe. I wil make ye daunce sutch a bloudy bargenet, as your whorish heate for euer shall be cooled . . . But I make to God a vow, that neuer wyll I take one sound and restful slepe, vntil I haue dispatched that infamous fact from our bloud, and that caitif whoremonger be vsed according to his desert.[32]

Belleforest's Antonio is essentially identical with Bandello's but not without occasional modifications. The translator is more explicit than his original about Antonio's manly virtues. They are repeatedly dwelt upon, and Belleforest once goes as far as stating that "Mayster Bologna was one of the wisest and most perfect Gentlemen that the land of Naples that tyme brought forth, and for his Beauty, Proportion, Gallantnesse, Valiaunce,

and good grace, without comparison." [33] Antonio's confusion
when the Duchess asks for his advice concerning her marriage is
stressed, as well as the gratitude and humility with which he
accepts her hand, all in perfect accordance with Bandello. But
there is more than a suspicion of selfishness in the thoughts and
behavior of Belleforest's hero. "Shall I be so voyde of wisdome to
suffer the yonge Princesse to see hirselfe contempned of mee,
thereby to conuert hir loue to teares, by setting hir mynde vpon
an other, that shall seek mine ouerthrow? Who knoweth not the
fury of a woman: specially the Noble dame, by seeing hirselfe
despised?" [34] Prudence can hardly be carried further.

After the marriage Antonio's conduct is the same in both
versions. He suggests his own flight to Ancona, firmly believing
that his is the only life in danger. When overtaken at Forlì he is
"Full of teares therefore, astonishment and feare," and not until
the Duchess implores him to save himself does he do so, "not
forgetting the money which she offred vnto him." [35] As in Bandello he is warned by Delio that people have been hired to kill
him, does not believe this and is murdered. His melancholy
recital in Milan, after which he "could not forbeare from pouring
forth his luke warme Tears, which abundantly ran downe his
heauy Face," is also an elaboration of a hint in the Italian
novella.[36]

The attitude taken by Belleforest to Antonio is obviously far
from consistent; as was to be expected it varies according to the
demands of the moral issue. Antonio as the master of the
Duchess' household is a prodigy of manly virtues; Antonio as a
pretender to his mistress' hand is "the simplest person of all the
trimmest Gentlemen of Naples"; Antonio as the victim of cruel
revenge is a touching and pathetic figure.[37] The incident that
decides Belleforest's attitude and gives a characteristic flavor to
his work is undoubtedly the marriage. It constitutes an outrageous breach of propriety and degree: a "household seruaunt"
is presumptious enough to "mount vpon a Prynces Bed." [38] For

such behavior, which Bandello passes by without comment, no words are too strong for Belleforest. Ambition now definitely enters among Antonio's motives.

It is undeniable that Belleforest makes Antonio's prudence look more like egoism, cowardice, and stupid irresolution than does Bandello. But, except where the marriage is concerned, this need not be the result of a deliberate change of attitude to the major-domo. It should be noted that, in spite of his predilection for moralizing, Belleforest never lets fall a disparaging remark about his character. A strain of sentimentality and a streak of ambition have been added; otherwise the translator does no more than follow up hints in his original. But because of Belleforest's habit of stating expressly and clumsily what Bandello only touches upon, the discrepancy between the first description of Antonio and his subsequent thoughts and deeds is now considerably more disturbing. Too many conflicting qualities may be attributed to the gentleman. In spite of the crudeness of Belleforest's art, his hero obviously contains the elements from which a subtle character study might be made.

Belleforest's attitude to the Duchess is similarly determined by her decision to marry, and his attempts at an analysis of her motives are thus of particular interest. Her thoughts are presented in detail: "a certayne vnacquainted lust" is fighting against her determination not to "degenerate from the royall bloud." [39] She falls violently in love with Antonio and conquers her reluctance to proposing herself by remembering his excellent qualities. Two things about this marriage are made abundantly clear. First, there can be no valid excuse for a duchess, particularly one of royal blood, to "couple hir selfe" with a man of Antonio's position in society. The fact that she is prepared to renounce her privileges and live as a simple gentlewoman only makes her case worse: she is at the same time evading her responsibilities.

Further, Belleforest takes great pains to enlighten his readers about the true nature of the secret wedding. It is nothing but

"a Maske and couerture to hide hir follies and shamelesse lusts." [40]
Even while the Duchess is explaining to Antonio her abhorrence
of love without marriage, she is "beholdinge him with a wanton
and luring eye." [41] Extenuating circumstances are not cited.
"Thys Lady waxed weary of lying alone, and gryeued hir Hearte
to be withoute a match, specially in the Nyght." [42] No analysis
could be less tolerant.

But this represents only one aspect of the Duchess' case. Belleforest also allows her to present her motives herself, and this she
does with considerable eloquence. An argument used by Bandello
in his preface to the novella is now resorted to by the Duchess:
"And what greater right haue Princes to ioyne wyth a simple
Gentlewoman, than the Princesse to mary a Gentleman, and
sutch as Anthonio Bologna is." [43] And once the relentless pursuit
of her is over and the executioners enter, the note of condemnation is forgotten. Her reaction to the warning of her impending
death is pitifully human: "hir cryes, and moanes together with
hir sighes and lamentations declared with what chere she
receyued the aduertisement." [44] She then begs the executioners
to spare her children and servant and turns to God to pray him
to forgive her sins. This prayer is, however, at the same time an
accusation. "I see wel that I haue trespassed against thy maiesty
in some more notoryous crime than in marriage." [45] She is neither
contrite nor repentant. "Is it a sinne to marry? Is it a fault to fly,
and auoide the sinne of Whoredome? What Lawes be these,
where marriage bed, and ioyned matrimony is pursued wyth lyke
seuerity, that Murder, Theft, and Aduoutry are? And what
Christianity in a Cardinall, to shed the bloud which hee ought to
defend?" [46]

This outburst reveals the reasons why Belleforest found it impossible to persist in complete condemnation of the Duchess.
Secret and sinful though her marriage is, it remains valid before
God and man, it is "absolute marriage." Further, some balance
between evil and, let us say, a lesser evil must be maintained in

the story. The vengeance of the Aragonian brothers being monstrously savage, the Duchess is bound to appear in a more and more favorable light. When she dies, she is not represented as overtaken by divine justice but as the victim of inhuman cruelty. She is innocent in her own eyes and allowed to defend herself with passion and ingenuity.

Belleforest's attitude to his heroine is thus by no means so biased as it seems at first sight. His preference for the monologue makes him present both sides of her case with commendable impartiality. Although he condemns the outrageous marriage of the lovers in terms of exceptional vehemence, this should not make us forget the excellent qualities with which these lovers are adorned. In spite of the sin of the Duchess—let us call it "a certayne vnacquaynted lust"—and the sin of Antonio—mainly indecorous ambition—they are both described as persons of some charm, considerable merit, and undeniable pathos.

Beard, Goulart, and Others

Painter's translation is not the only Elizabethan account of the life and death of the Duchess. Brief references to her choice of husband occur in *The Forrest of Fancy* (1579) and Greene's *Gwydonius; the Carde of Fancie* (1584), in which works Antonio is called Ulrico and the Duchess commended for her unconventional marriage.[47] The way in which Greene cites her case is characteristic: in Gwydonius' eloquent efforts to persuade Princess Castania to marry him, the Duchess is invoked as one of the ladies who have created precedents by loving, and, in her case, marrying their inferiors. "They madame, respected the man, & not their money, their wills, & not their wealth, their loue, not their liuings: their constancie, not their coine: their person, not their parentage: and the inward vertue, not the outward value." [48] Although by such arguments Gwydonius finally wins his beloved's heart without revealing his princely birth, her father is less open to persuasion, and an intrigue of some complexity becomes necessary before the story is brought to a happy close.

Whetstone's reflections on the marriage of the Duchess of Amalfi in *An Heptameron of Ciuill Discourses* (1582) are more detailed and immediately relevant:

The *Cardinal* of *Aragon,* aduenged the base choice of his Sister, the Duchess of *Malfy,* with the death of her selfe, her Children, and her Husband: and alleadged in defence, that he had done no iniurie to Nature, but purged his House of dishonour: for Nature (quoth hee) is perfect, and who blemisheth her is a monster in Nature, whose head, without wrong to Nature may be cut off.

Yea (quoth Soranso) but, this Cardinall, for all his habit, and glose of Justice, is for this Act, so often regestred for a Tirant, as I feare mee he will neuer come among ye nu[m]ber of Saints. But the example of these Mariages are vsuall, and such ensuing vengeaunce is but rare, and besides her espetiall contentment, a woman looseth none of her general titles of dignitie by matching w' her inferior.[49]

This passage occurs in the Fifth Day's Exercise in the *Heptameron,* in which "the inconueniences of ouer lofty, and too base Loue" are discussed, and it should be noted that the author concludes his argument in a manner considerably less favorable to the Duchess. Thus the difference between Whetstone's position and Belleforest's to the question of the secret and indecorous marriage is not so striking as it at first appears.

Thomas Beard's treatment of the subject in *The Theatre of Gods Judgements* (1597), where Belleforest's drastically condensed narrative appears under the heading "Of whoredomes committed vnder Colour of Marriage," is much more uncompromising.[50] Antonio, the Duchess, their three children, the chambermaid, and the Aragonian brothers are the only characters mentioned. The validity of the ceremony *per verba de praesenti* is not recognized, and the lovers are consequently described as living together in sin. Their perambulations are simplified: they flee from Naples to Ancona, from Ancona to Tuscany and then towards Venice, being overtaken somewhere on the road. Bologna alone escapes to Milan; his wife, the children, and the chamber-maid are strangled in Naples by "her brothers gard." For Antonio's death the Cardinal is made solely responsible, no doubt because of the rare opportunity that such a version gave Beard to inveigh against the sins of popes and cardinals. Nevertheless he insists in regarding the death of the lovers as an instance of God's justice, the Cardinal being used "as an instrument to punish those who vnder the vaile of secret marriage thought it lawfull for them to commit any villany." [51]

Simon Goulart's version, as translated by Grimeston in *Admirable and Memorable Histories* (1607), is considerably more detailed than Beard's and contain's Belleforest's plot almost un-abridged.[52] Gone, however, are the interminable dialogues and soliloquies and, to a great extent, also the moral reflections. No mention is made of the proposal of the Duchess, nor of the chambermaid's advice to escape by way of Loreto. Only scanty information is given about Antonio's sojourn in Milan. The same characters are introduced as in Beard, with the addition of the suborned murderer of Antonio, "a certaine Lombard a Captaine of a companie of foote." [53] Antonio is the only person mentioned by name.

The author's attitude to his main characters is easily defined. No word of censure is uttered against the Aragonian brothers, while the guilt of the lovers is painted in extremely dark colors. Instead of allowing the Duchess to excuse herself by complaining of the lack of acceptable suitors, as in Bandello and Belleforest, Goulart expressly states that partners "fitte for her qualitie . . . might easily haue beene found neere or farre off." [54] The only comments he makes on her character and behavior refer to her unchaste desires. Antonio is similarly treated. Nothing is said about his accomplishments, while he is roundly condemned for being presumptious, lustful and of mean estate. It is finally inter-esting to note that Goulart's Lombard captain uses a whole troop of soldiers to finish off Antonio, and also that the son of his victim is "forced to flie out of *Milan,* to change his name, and to retier himselfe farre off, where he died unknowne."[55]

This brings the list of English references to the Duchess of Amalfi to a close. Although convincing verbal evidence cannot be cited, there is little doubt that they are all ultimately derived from Belleforest–Painter and do not presuppose a knowledge of Bandello's Italian original or of the historical facts. Considering the great popularity of *The Palace of Pleasure,* this is hardly surprising. A good indication of this popularity is, I believe, established by a comparison between Painter's story of the Duchess and Barnabe Riche's tale of Sappho of Mantona (1581), a comparison that is of special interest in this connection.[56]

Duke Sappho is living in exile with his family, and his son Silvanus, now a servant at the court of the Duke of Vasconia, falls in love with his master's daughter Valeria. She returns his passion and ponders her position at length. Her words have a strangely familiar quality:

Alas (saieth she) is it possible, that now force perforce my mynde should bee so altered, that straying from the boundes and limites of vowed Chastitie: I should now become amourous, and subiect to a certaine vnacquainted luste . . . it behoueth me to shewe my self, as issued forthe of the noble house of *Vasconya* . . . Then the partie whom I loue, is both vertuous, valiant, sage, of good grace, learned and wise . . . It is *Siluanus* whom I loue, and of hym I pretende to make a lawfull housbande, for otherwise I detest to leade the filthie life of lawlesse luste . . . *Siluanus* therefore shalbee my loyall housbande, meanyng thereby neither to offende God nor ma[n].[57]

What follows is the story of the Duchess of Malfi, although with considerable variations; whole passages are lifted from Painter and put into the mouths of Valeria and her beloved. Having a real prince for his hero, however, has forced Riche somewhat to modify his characterization; it is Silvanus who delivers the spirited defense of marriage beginning "Is it a synne to Marrie, is it a faulte to flye and auoyde the synne of whore-

dome?"[58] In spite of the furious outburst of the Duke of
Vasconia—"I vowe I will neuer take sou[n]d nor restfull slepe,
vntill I haue dispatched that infamous facte from our blood, and
that villaine whoremonger with his trull be vsed accordyng to
their desertes"—all difficulties are finally overcome and a complete reconciliation is achieved.[59] If Webster was interested in
variations on Bandello's theme, some were immediately at hand.

Lope de Vega

To include a Spanish play, not printed until 1618 and never
translated into English, among the possible sources of *The
Duchess of Malfi* may appear superfluous. A case, however, has
been made for Webster's dependence on *El Mayordomo de la
Duquesa de Amalfi,* and the similarities are sufficiently striking
to justify an examination of Lope's tragedy.[60] Its main source is
Bandello's novella, from which it takes most of its plot, some
significant details and most characters. Occasionally the Italian
prose seems to have been translated almost literally into Spanish
verse. What concerns us here is, however, the obvious deviations
from Bandello.

The simple plot of the Italian story is complicated by the introduction of a new character, Urbino Castelvetro, secretary to the
Duchess, on whose conduct the outcome of the play largely
depends. He suspects Antonio of carrying on an intrigue with
Libia, the Duchess' chambermaid, with whom he himself is in
love, and thus has reason to keep a close watch on Antonio. He
discovers that the major-domo has a child in his care and concludes that Libia must be its mother, whereupon he hastens to
communicate his discovery to the Duchess. She understands that
it is only a matter of time before the true facts will be known
and arranges a solemn dismissal of Antonio on account of his
alleged scandalous behavior. When Urbino relates this incident
to Otavio de Medicis, who has long been a suitor for the Duchess'
hand, this gentleman realizes at once who is the mother of the

child, and the Duchess' secret is out. The relieved Urbino stays with Libia in the Duchess' service and they are both captured with her.

Urbino's final task in the play is to lure Antonio from Milan back to Amalfi, and he performs this without realizing its implications. Otavio, on the other hand, is well aware of the fate that awaits Antonio and is willing to participate in dispatching him. He is not, however, prepared to satisfy the demands of honor by murdering the Duchess and her children. This is done on the orders of her brother Julio de Aragón (the Cardinal is not included among the dramatis personae) and both Otavio and the young Duke of Amalfi are furious at this outrage. The Duke's solemn vow of revenge for his mother's death brings the play to a close.

Apart from the deviations that the Urbino-Libia-Otavio by-plot makes necessary, Lope changes or adds little. In the wooing scene he makes the Duchess twice ask the hesitant Antonio to put on his hat in order to make him understand that she wants him to address her as his equal. The couple is then married in church, properly and irrevocably although in disguise, and their children are brought up by peasants. Of Antonio's visit to Naples before leaving for Ancona, an episode mentioned in passing by Bandello, Lope makes a stay of two years, with frequent nightly excursions to Amalfi. He does not mention the expulsion of the lovers from Ancona, nor their sojourn in Siena. The letters referred to in Bandello, in which Antonio is told that his troubles will soon be over, are actually produced in the Spanish play; one of them is from Julio de Aragón and promises life and security to Antonio and his family, provided they leave Italy.

This letter brings about the catastrophe. Antonio returns to Amalfi eager to join his wife and children and to depart with them in peace. He is received coldly but politely by Julio, who gives him his hand to kiss. Poisoned by the glove he is led off the stage to die. The Duchess enters, exchanges a few words with

Julio and the young Duke, a door is thrown open and the heads of Antonio and the children are displayed on three plates. After a pitiful lamentation, the Duchess, also poisoned on Julio's orders, falls dead.

The attitude of the author to his characters and their deeds makes a few comments necessary. Without forgetting to make the tenderness of the Duchess' bearing to her husband and children evident to all spectators, Lope took some pains to stress her rank, dignity and royal descent. She meets her brother as his equal and delivers a spirited denial of his right to hold her prisoner. Antonio, on the other hand, kneels to Julio and kisses his hand. The contrast is the more remarkable inasmuch as Antonio is not described as a man of ignoble family. He is "hijodalgo," but unworthy of such a great lady.[61]

It is difficult to say whether the fate that overtakes the lovers and their children is represented as just punishment or cruel revenge. The concept of family honor is undoubtedly important here as in so many of Lope's dramas, and we should think twice before pronouncing Julio de Aragón the villain of the play. He acts as the head of a noble family, and his motives are admittedly legitimate. But in spite of this reservation it is impossible not to note that Lope hints at other possible solutions to this dilemma of honor. Otavio wants to see Antonio killed but wishes to spare the Duchess and the children. Julio himself suggests banishment as the proper penalty for them all. The young Duke of Amalfi calls Antonio father, and his half brother Alejandro calls Julio uncle. Lope may have left the question of human justice open. He knew perfectly well, however, what would be the divine judgment.

II ✦ *Potential Secondary Sources*

Sidney's Arcadia

It has long been known that in *The Duchess of Malfi* Webster derived many ideas and expressions from Sir Philip Sidney's *Arcadia*, occasionally borrowing phrases almost word for word.[1] This undeniable fact makes it probable that he was also influenced by Sidney in his treatment of situation and character. Although most of the episodes in the book have no bearing on *The Duchess of Malfi* and many similarities that exist between other episodes and incidents in the play should be explained as accidental, there are cases where a close comparison between Sidney and Webster may prove rewarding. It might thus be argued that in the Musidorus-Pamela story, one of the important themes of *Arcadia*, the similarity to Webster's main plot is too great to allow us to dismiss it as pure coincidence.

Prince Musidorus disguises himself as a shepherd in order to serve his beloved Pamela, Princess of Arcadia, and succeeds in making a favorable impression on her. When it comes to declaring his love, however, he finds himself at a disadvantage because of their apparently unequal social status. He more than suspects that Pamela is in love with him and soon makes her realize who he actually is. This difficulty overcome, the lovers are content for a while to exchange words and looks, Pamela occasionally treating her prince as the servant he pretends to be. Finally they decide to leave Arcadia in secret, with the intention of getting married as soon as possible. But on their way to the coast they are overtaken; Musidorus defends his beloved with remarkable fury but is forced to surrender, and the couple are imprisoned, partly at least for their gross breach of propriety. Whether Musidorus is a prince or a shepherd, whether his intentions are honorable or not, the abduction of a princess is a matter on which he can be tried for his life.

So far the similarities between this story and that of the Duchess are admittedly vague. Marriages between persons of unequal rank were after all among the common scandals in Elizabethan and Jacobean England. It is, however, relevant to note that Sidney's narrative leads up to a familiar situation, one in which he seems almost to specialize, the behavior of young ladies in prison. This time a very melancholy note is struck: Pamela and her sister Philoclea, who is in similar trouble, weep pitifully while awaiting the execution of their lovers, "Although no doubte their faces, did rather beautifie sorrow, then sorrow coulde darken that, which even in darkenes did shine." [2] Even the proud and disdainful Pamela finds comfort in tears.

Their behavior is in sharp contrast to the constancy with which, in another episode in *Arcadia,* the Lycian Queen Erona endures her imprisonment. "*Erona* sadde indeede, yet like one rather used, then new fallen to sadnesse (as who had the joyes of her hart alreadie broken) seemed rather to welcome then to shunne that ende of miserie." [3] Her beauty is perceived "more perfectly in wo, then in joyfulnesse," and she finds "the world but a wearisom stage unto her, where she played a part against her will." [4]

These two prison scenes are relatively minor incidents in Sidney's book, particularly when compared to the prolonged torture to which Pamela and Philoclea have previously been subjected at the hands of the wicked Queen Cecropia. When flattery and cunning can make neither of the sisters consent to marrying Amphialus, the Queen's son, she has them mercilessly whipped and, when this only makes them obdurate, she proceeds to "giving them terrors, sometimes with noices of horror, sometimes with suddaine frightings in the night, when the solitary darkenesse thereof might easier astonish the disarmed senses." [5]

When this also fails, Cecropia forces Philoclea to watch the execution of a lady who is apparently her sister. Similar measures are tried on Pamela: Philoclea's head is displayed to her, lying seemingly severed from the body in a basin of gold. These horrors break the resistance of the sisters so completely that they only wish to die, Pamela even going so far as to refuse to eat. In order to keep them alive—since without bride there will be no wedding for her son—Cecropia has to reveal how she has tricked them. When Amphialus realizes how the prisoners have been treated, he turns against his mother and searches for her, sword in hand, filled with "the horriblest despaire, which a most guiltie conscience could breed, with wild lookes promising some terrible issue." [6] In her efforts to escape, Cecropia, who is now preparing a poison for the sisters, falls over a balustrade and is killed, whereupon her son stabs himself to death.

Another passage in *Arcadia* which must obviously be included among Webster's potential sources, although it has nothing to do with princesses in love or in distress, is the echo eclogue. [7] Since, however, the device is old and not uncommon in sixteenth-century literature, other possible sources of inspiration should also be listed. There are at least half a dozen earlier or contemporary plays in which echo scenes occur. In *Old Fortunatus* such an episode opens the play, the echo carrying on a would-be funny conversation with Fortunatus, simply repeating the last two or three words of every sentence he utters. [8] A considerably more ingenious echo comments on Academico's situation in the second part of *The Return from Parnassus*. It plays on words (come by it—Buy it; fortunate as hee—Asse he) and twists them conveniently (gold here—Cold cheare; worship—Words cheape), all with a decidedly farcical intent. [9] But considering the nature of the original Echo legend, it is not surprising that the device should also have been used to tinge a scene with sadness rather than to provoke laughter. Jonson introduces a mournful nymph in *Cynthia's Revels* but without letting her act the part in earnest. In *The Wounds of Civil War* and *The Hog hath Lost his Pearl,* on the other hand, the echo is used to provide despairing heroes with proper melancholy answers, repeating such words as "grief" and "death," but in the end giving some hope of a happier future.[10] Except in *Old Fortunatus,* the conversation is carried on almost exclusively by question and answer, a device which must have set off all these scenes as highly conventional from the very beginning.

This aspect is quite legitimately further developed in Sidney's eclogue, which is after all a mock echo scene, a command performance before King Basilius. Not only does the echo answer each question faithfully, but the interrogator repeats the answer, the poem being thus woven together into a rigid verbal pattern of remarkable artificiality. In spite of some ominous answers by the echo, the note of melancholy that is supposed to reign is only occasionally predominant. At least one line might, however, have had a direct appeal to the author of *The Duchess of Malfi:*

> What great name may I give so heav'nly a woman.
> A wo-man.[11]

Herodotus and Cinthio

In 1954 Mario Praz pointed out that the similarity between the final episode in Herodotus' story of the Egyptian King Rampsinitus and the young thief and Ferdinand's trick of the dead man's hand in *The Duchess of Malfi* was too striking to be accidental.[12] The story exists in two almost identical sixteenth-century versions, both of which may well have been available to Webster: one in B. R.'s translation of Herodotus (1584), and the other in Bandello, where it forms the twenty-fifth novella of part one, the one immediately preceding that of the Duchess of Amalfi.[13]

Because of this intriguing juxtaposition I have used Bandello's version as the basis for my remarks on Herodotus' story.

There is in fact very little to say. Not until the young thief, equipped with the arm of an executed murderer, is approaching the bed of the King's daughter, does a situation occur which even faintly recalls a scene from Webster's play. But now: "volendo l'ardita fanciulla porgli addosso le mani, lo scaltrito giovine le porse il troncato braccio dell'assassino, e via se ne fuggì, lasciando quella di spavento piena e di meraviglia, perciocchè ella si pensava al ladro avere strappato il braccio." [14] It is also worth noting that the astute young man is forgiven by the King and allowed to marry his daughter. "Così questo fratricida e ladrone di vil sangue nato, divenne barone e signore di gentiluomini." [15]

Of such an episode there is no trace in *El Mayordomo de la Duquesa de Amalfi*, although Lope adds decapitations and a gruesome display of gory heads to the horrors of the final act. There was of course no shortage of material of this kind in the literature commonly available to Renaissance dramatists, the banquets of Thyestes and Astyages being perhaps the most notable examples. Similar effects are also used in Giraldi Cinthio's well-known tragedy of *Orbecche,* in which, moreover, the grim consequence of a secret marriage between a princess and her father's most valued servant are delineated. Although this Senecan tragedy is of a scope too limited to have been of much use to Lope, there is reason to believe that the horror devices as well as other details in the Spanish play were suggested by a reading, not of the tragedy but of the novella of Orbecche, which appears in Cinthio's *Ecatommiti* under the title *Oronte allevato in basso stato ama Orbecche figliuola del re di Persia.*[16] If the story was one of Lope's sources, it may also have been one of Webster's.

Oronte, although of royal descent, has been brought up in humble circumstances but, being "bellissimo e di leggiadre maniere ornato, e pieno di tante virtù," he makes a spectacular career at the Persian court, where he becomes the right hand of

King Sulmone.[17] He and the King's daughter Orbecche fall in love but keep their feelings secret for a while, having sufficient delight in admiring each other, she "il primo cavaliere del mondo" and he "la più mirabil cosa, che potesse vedere occhio mortale." [18] At last the Princess can remain silent no longer and, "tutta di nobile vergogna vermiglia divenuta," discloses her love to Oronte in a long speech, ending by proposing a secret marriage.[19] Oronte's love for her overcomes his sense of duty to his master and he accepts her hand. She calls for her nurse and chambermaid and in their presence gives Oronte a ring and exchanges vows with him. Their happiness is undisturbed for some time, although the existence of a hidden passage between the King's rooms and his daughter's must have been a source of anxiety to them. Then a Parthian prince asks Sulmone for Orbecche's hand. She is alarmed, turns to her nurse and Oronte for advice, and together they resolve to flee to Armenia. They make the court believe that they are only going to a pleasure resort in the vicinity of the capital, and once there they easily escape. Sulmone brings pressure to bear on the Armenian king to make him send the fugitives back, but for nine years his efforts to get them into his power are in vain. At last he sends a conciliatory letter to Oronte, in which he promises him great honors if he returns. Oronte does so, is made governor of a rich city, and writes a letter to his wife telling her and their two boys to join him in Persia. On his next visit to the King he is taken prisoner and strangled.

When Orbecche and the children arrive, Sulmone proceeds with his revenge. The children are separated from their mother and stabbed to death, whereupon Orbecche is invited to the royal chamber. On her entry Sulmone informs her that he has prepared a gift for her as a token of their reconciliation, and Oronte's head and the children's bodies, the daggers still in the wounds, are displayed to her. The King is not, however, allowed to gloat over his revenge for long. Orbecche pulls a dagger from the throat of one of the boys, who at this gives a last groan, and plunges it into Sulmone's heart. She then cuts off his head, puts it on the same plate as her husband's and kills herself, falling covered with blood on the bleeding corpses of her children.

Cinthio makes it clear from the very first what moral lesson he wants to teach the reader of his novella; his intention is to show "that children ought to honor their parents, and that the servants of kings ought to serve their masters faithfully, and that kings ought not to break faith with those who trust them." [20] This might lead us to expect either an essay in the calm Bandellian art of storytelling, or an effort to moralize on whatever aberration from virtue and decency that takes place, a product similar to Belleforest's. But Cinthio chooses neither alternative. His impartiality is really counterfeit. By stating in so many words that King Sulmone is a cruel and unnatural tyrant, he evades the moral issue he would otherwise have to face and is free to bestow all his sympathy on the unfortunate lovers. The result is that their breach of faith is forgotten, while Sulmone's revenge appears truly ferocious. The supposed base descent of Oronte does not make his conduct outrageous: Sulmone himself defends him against detractors, pronouncing him—before the marriage— "degno figliuolo di ogni gran re." [21] When after the flight of the lovers Sulmone demands their extradition, the King of Armenia makes an eloquent speech in their defense, in which he refers to the secret marriage as a "peccato d'amore," which should be pardoned rather than punished.[22] In his opinion such unequal matches are clearly allowed, both according to the evidence of history and the voice of common sense: it is greatness of spirit and royal virtues that make a man "degno d'impero," not riches and titles.[23] Thus there is nothing ambiguous about Cinthio's attitude to his characters. Although his story is based on a rebellion against both paternal and royal authority, certainly a more formidable combination than the one in Bandello, his sympathy is all on the side of the rebels.

Various Other Possibilities

In this lengthy description of possible sources of *The Duchess of Malfi* no mention has so far been made of any document containing references to lycanthropy, the strange disease from which Webster makes Duke Ferdinand suffer in the last act of the play. The probable source of inspiration was, however, a very familiar work, Goulart's *Admirable and Memorable Histories,* in which several pages are devoted to a discussion of this affliction:

> For there be *Licanthropes* in whom the melancholike humor doth so rule, as they imagine themselues to be transformed into Wolues . . . and all night doe nothing but runne into Church-yardes, and about graues . . . one of these melancholike *Licanthropes* . . . carried then vpon his soulders the whole thigh and legge of a dead man . . . A Countri-man neere vnto *Pauia,* in the yeare 1541 . . . did constantlye affirme that hee was a Wolfe, and that there was no other difference, but that Wolues were commonlie hayrie without, and hee was betwixt the skinne and the flesh. Some (too barbarous and cruell Wolues in effect) desiring to trie the truth thereof, gave him manie wounds vpon the armes and legges.[24]

The resemblance between this passage and *The Duchess of Malfi,* V, ii, 7–20, is so striking as to settle the question of Webster's source immediately: the dramatist knew Goulart's work and derived material from it when he wrote *The Duchess of Malfi.* Similarly, the close parallels between passages in Whetstone's *Heptameron* and a number of lines in the tragedy put his knowledge of that work beyond doubt.[25]

Admirable and Memorable Histories may also account for the introduction of Pescara as one of the commanders of the imperial army in *The Duchess of Malfi* and the honorable disposition of this Websterian character. Not only does "Ferdinand d'Avalos Marquis of Pescara, Lieutenant to the Emperour Charles 5. in the Duchie of Milan" appear in Goulart, but reference is also made to Alfonso, his successor as Marquis of Pescara, "running vp and downe the streetes to preuent the wrong they went about to offer to the honour of Women," an incident, however, which occurred at the sack of Rome, not in connection with the battle of Pavia.[26]

This is of course not to say that Webster cannot have noticed a reference to Pescara elsewhere; it is in fact extremely probable that he had, since Lannoy, "He that had the honour Of taking the *French* King Prisoner" (III, iii, 7–8), is mentioned in *The Duchess of Malfi* without appearing in Goulart at all. The obvious source for such additional information was Guicciardini's *Storia d'Italia* (translated by Fenton, 1579), where Lannoy is referred to in the proper place.[27] From this work other details tending to facilitate the shift in time from 1505–1513 to 1504–1525 that Webster made could also be derived. It might indeed be argued that a knowledge of Guicciardini should be presupposed for a dramatist bent upon dramatizing an episode in early sixteenth-century Italian history. The villainies of the Borgias, the exploits of Julius II, the murder of the warlike Cardinal Alidosi—apart from the collections of novelle there cannot have been many books that had more rewarding dramatic material to offer.

There is actually a strange parallel between the conduct of Webster's Cardinal and that of a prominent churchman contemporary with Lodovico d'Aragona, particularly in Guicciardini's version. "Cardinal *S. Severin* . . . a braue and valiant Cardinall bearing more inclinacion to armes then to holy exercises and contemplacions of religion, And lesse giuen to the vocacion of the church or ciuill or priuat profession, then to publike action and warlike imitacion," rode at the head of the French troops in the battle of Ravenna, "armed withall from toppe to toe with glittering armes," and "performed farre better the office of a Capteine then of a Cardinall or Legate."[28] And not only that; together with another Cardinal of a similar cast of mind he renounced his holy office and was forced to ask for a ceremony of reinstatement, a humiliation to which he submitted under the successor to the Pope against whom he had fought.[29]

Guicciardini's history was one of the important books of the

Elizabethan period, widely read and several times reprinted. It would be hazardous to approach the history of Webster's own age in the same confident spirit and attempt to determine his debt, not to printed sources but to particular historical episodes. Mr. Lucas has pointed out the similarities between the Duchess' case and that of Lady Arabella Stuart, without insisting that Webster had them in mind.[30] I believe that this attitude is right. The theory that the Elizabethan dramatists intended their plays to provide detailed commentaries on contemporary events has not been proved. But commentary is one thing, allusion another. It has long been suspected that Antonio's first speech in *The Duchess of Malfi* refers to Louis XIII's removal from the French court of the Maréchal d'Ancre, his wife, and their adherents, in 1617, the whole passage having been inserted at a revival of the play shortly after the event.[31] Concini's nationality, humble origin, and proud and insolent behavior seem to have made him generally detested, and the enthusiasm that greeted the news of his murder not only in France but also in England was remarkable. Seen against this background the addition of some fifteen lines, of questionable relevance and strikingly Chapmanesque, to the first scene of *The Duchess of Malfi* would be understandable.[32]

Are there other possible interpolations in the play, perhaps referring to the same sequence of events? This is hardly a question to which a valid answer can be given now, but the following incident in Concini's career, to which other contemporary pamphlets also allude, should undoubtedly be recorded:

quand pour jouer au dit billiard, il se couvrit devant sa Majesté, et après lui disoit: "Sire, Votre Majesté me permettra bien de me couvrir"; cependant il l'avait déjà fait, et que Sa Majesté, n'avoit pas laissé de lui dire assez longtemps après: "Oui, couvrez-vous." [33]

This reference to a behavior that caused considerable stir at the French court clearly recalls Antonio's and the Duchess' conversation on the desirability of introducing a similar habit at the Ducal court of Amalfi; the Concini episode may conceivably have drawn Webster's attention to this question of etiquette.

The doffing of the hat is, however, a time-honored show of courtesy from inferiors to superiors, and scenes in which it occurs or is described are frequent in the Elizabethan drama, usually on a strict servant-to-master level and without any possible allusion to current events.[34] The more ceremonious occasions are few, but of particular interest. Listen to Mugeron commenting on Monsieur d'Olive's concept of an ambassador's rights:

> ... he stands on this,
> That when he once hath kissed your Highness' hand
> And taken his despatch, he then presents
> Your Highness' person, hath your place and power,
> Must put his hat on, use you as you him;
> That you may see before he goes how well
> He can assume your presence and your greatness.[35]

This is no parallel to the Duchess' suggestion to Antonio, but it shows that the question was not irrelevant in court circles and, if we may believe Chapman, least of all irrelevant in France. Other dramatists agree with him. In Act III of Fletcher's *The Noble Gentleman* a brief exchange between Shatillion and Mount-Marine's wife indicates that a loyal Frenchman was expected to remove his hat at the very sound of the King's name, and in *Love's Labours Lost* Armado's reprimand to Holofernes— "I do beseech thee, remember thy courtesy"—which is followed by the permission to "apparel thy head," should undoubtedly be interpreted in the same way.[36] But everyone in France did not look favorably upon this show of reverence to the sovereign. In his essay "Of Sumptuarie Lawes" Montaigne draws attention to various obnoxious customs of recent date that he would like to see abolished, and among them he enumerates "that, against our forefathers manner, and the particular liberties of our *French* nobilitie, we should stand bare-headed, aloofe-off from them, wheresoever they be"—thus insisting on the same ancient privilege to which Webster makes the Duchess refer:[37]

> DUCH. I have heard you say, that the French Courtiers
>   Weare their hats on fore the King.
> ANT. I have seene it.
> DUCH. In the Presence?
> ANT. Yes:
> DUCH. Why should not we bring up that fashion?
>
> (II, i, 121–126)

If the origin of the episode is French, a more plausible source than Montaigne's essay cannot be imagined.

So much for the description of the works that may have had an important bearing on the basic story of *The Duchess of Malfi,* on what Webster added and the direction in which he developed it. The selection of "potential secondary sources" is necessarily somewhat arbitrary: to describe all the works from which Webster may have derived information is out of the question. The stress is moreover consistently on story, on dramatic material, not on verbal or poetic inspiration, and thus no discussion of Alexander's *Monarchicke Tragedies,* Elyot's *Image of Gouernance,* or Matthieu's *The Heroyk Life and Deplorable Death of the Most Christian King Henry the Fourth,* is called for.[38] The works of Montaigne are, however, in a special category, at least for the purposes of this study.[39] It is inconceivable that Webster could have read the *Essays,* jotted down and refashioned lines that struck his fancy and then closed his mind completely to the attitudes to which Montaigne gives expression. The bearing of the *Essays* on *The Duchess of Malfi* will not be insisted on here, but they will be taken for granted as part of Webster's intellectual background and thus be referred to repeatedly in the analysis of the meaning of the play for which we shall soon be ready.

III ❧ *Analysis of the Documents*

Toward a Theory: Verbal Evidence

It is obviously impossible to state with perfect confidence which of our potential sources Webster actually used. The mind of the dramatist remains an unknown quantity between source and play: we may collect documents but we do not know Webster's interpretation of them. In our first approach to the problem we might, however, do worse than to adopt the method by means of which Webster's knowledge of *Arcadia,* Montaigne, and others has been proved, i.e., look for lines in *The Duchess of Malfi* that were certainly borrowed from the documents described above. But considering the nature of these—two of them are in Italian, one in Spanish, and the others in English often awkward—the inquiry has not been limited to the search for obvious verbal echoes but also includes cases of probable non-literal borrowing, where the theme of a passage rather than its words seems to have set the dramatist's mind working. An investigation along such lines might be expected to yield some indications, if not positive proof, as to which documents Webster relied on.

These expectations are at least partly fulfilled when Painter's version in *The Palace of Pleasure* is examined, for, as Sampson already noted, there are several lines in *The Duchess of Malfi* that can be traced back to expressions in Painter.[1] But on the whole these verbal echoes are surprisingly few and very seldom of the striking kind that a study of *Arcadia* can furnish. The borrowings from Sidney are often obvious, indeed almost literal: "It is weakenes too much to remember what should have beene done"; "our state is soncke below the degree of feare"; "He with an angry voice asked, Who was there? A poore Gentlewoman (answered the partie) that wish long life unto you. And I soone death to you (said he) for the horrible curse you have given me." [2]

There are two or three passages in *The Duchess of Malfi* whose origin in Belleforest–Painter is recognizable in the same unmistakable way: "We may confesse also these brutall brethren to be more butcherly than euer Otho Erle of Monferrato, and prince of Vrbin was, who caused a yeoman of his chamber to be wrapped in a sheete poudred with sulpher and brimstone, and afterwards kindled with a Candle"; "we be still bound to the chaine like the Galley slaue"—these strike a note that at once suggests famous lines in Webster.[3] Other cases are clear but of less immediate effect: "Alas . . . am I happed into so straunge misery, that with mine owne mouth I must make request to him, which with all humility ought to offer mee hys service"; "I thinke if I should descend into Hell, they would know, whither any shadowe there were in loue with me." [4] Some other examples may be adduced but are on the whole unconvincing. Webster's debt to Belleforest–Painter is not primarily one of phraseology.

And yet, in the search for verbal echoes it is almost impossible not to stumble on definite proof, although of a slightly different kind, that Webster not only knew but made good use of Belleforest–Painter's "nouel." In the frantic outburst of the Cardinal's brother and the description of the chambermaid's death—passages that were quoted above in Chapter I—the actual words used may not anticipate phrases in *The Duchess of Malfi,* but the ideas and emotions expressed have been adapted by Webster with remarkable care and given a new and significant shape.[5] Other cases of the same kind occur, but those now referred to are indeed so illuminating that they are impossible to ignore for anyone who has taken the trouble of reading Belleforest's "nouel."

A borrowing of ideas rather than of phrases—the conclusion should perhaps have been expected. Painter has none of Sidney's gift of felicitous or at least quaint expressions. Very little verbal inspiration can be derived from his pages. Nor should we anticipate many echoes in *The Duchess of Malfi* from the short, matter-of-fact versions of Beard and Goulart. There are in fact none from the former and only an extremely doubtful one from the latter work.[6] But Bandello's Italian original might present a different case. Conversation fills a considerable part of it, and it is written in a style that is a fit medium for artistic expression. Yet there are very few lines in Webster that suggest phrases in Bandello rather than in Belleforest. The Duchess' "This woman's of my Councell" (I, i, 546) seems closer to "una figliuola . . . la quale ella già aveva dei suoi pensieri fatta consapevole" than to "one onely Gentlewoman which . . . was made priuy to the heauy mariage."[7] Ferdinand's

> Foolish men,
> That ere will trust their honour in a Barke,
> Made of so slight, weake bull-rush, as is woman,
> Apt every minnit to sinke it!

> (II, v, 46–49)

may also, as Mr. Lucas points out, have been suggested by "E nel vero grave sciocchezza quella degli uomini mi pare, che vogliono che l'onor loro e di tutta la casata consista nel' appetito d'una donna" in Bandello's preface to the Duchess' story, particularly as no similar expression is to be found in Belleforest.[8] But the parallels are vague and certainly do not warrant even such a cautious statement as that Webster *probably* knew Bandello in the Italian original.

The only verbal evidence to suggest that he really had such knowledge is indirect: it is the manner in which he seems to have elaborated in *The Duchess of Malfi* the reference to the ability of one of the Aragonian brothers to "menar le mani." Although the phrase is ambiguous, the testimony of the Corona manuscripts makes it plain that it refers to the soldierly qualities of the

Cardinal Lodovico d'Aragona of history, qualities of which Bandello cannot have been ignorant.[9] Whether the corresponding characteristics of the Cardinal of the play can be satisfactorily explained if the phrase is supposed to have been unknown to Webster, will be discussed later. For the time being we have to admit that this may be an example of how a reference in Bandello —and not in his translators—has been developed by the dramatist.

An examination of the other major non-English sources that have been suggested, Cinthio's Orbecche novella and Lope de Vega's *El Mayordomo,* yields a similar result. There are no lines in *The Duchess of Malfi* that are obviously derived from Cinthio and only very few that even faintly suggest such an origin; the repeated references to Antonio as "basely descended," "a base mind," "this base, low fellow" may be renderings of Cinthio's equally persistent phrase "di basso stato," but this is obviously too insignificant a parallel to be taken seriously. The possible echoes from Lope are also unsatisfactory, with one notable exception: the request of the Duchess to Antonio to put on his hat in her presence, thus setting a new fashion to the court.[10] This, as well as his polite refusal, certainly recalls the repeated "Cubrete" of Lope's Duchess and his Antonio's efforts to evade the issue. Although the episodes occur in quite different scenes, although Webster stresses that the Duchess' request is based on French precedents, and although the similarity is one of situation rather than of phrasing, the parallel seems too striking to be accidental.

The cases of "Cubrete" and "menar le mani" are unique. Further inquiry makes it plain that, even though we make every allowance for the strange expressions to which a Spanish or Italian phrase may have given rise in a Jacobean dramatist's mind, these are the only sentences in the non-English works under consideration that seem to have left any mark in *The Duchess of Malfi*. But this does not prove that Webster knew Lope and Bandello. What is put beyond doubt by a study of the phraseology of *The Duchess of Malfi* and its possible sources is only the fact that Webster knew and made good use of Painter's twenty-third "nouel" and Sidney's *Arcadia*. There are also slight indications that he might have had access to Bandello's novella I: 26 and some knowledge of Lope's *El Mayordomo de la Duquesa de Amalfi*, but this is a question that needs further study before a definite answer is attempted. As to Beard's and Cinthio's stories, the lack of convincing or even probable echoes from these works makes their inclusion among Webster's sources seem hazardous and only to be recommended if strong evidence, hitherto not produced, should demand it. But Goulart's version of the Duchess' life and Whetstone's references to her must be accepted as known to Webster even without the existence of good verbal parallels between the relevant passages and the play.[11]

The Main Source and Its Limitations

The conclusion that we do not know whether Webster used other sources than those we have always known he used, is hardly to be considered satisfactory. It provides us, however, with a sound basis for further investigation. Restricting this to the material established as Webster's sources, it is possible to compare these documents with the finished play and thus to decide the dramatist's debt to Belleforest and Sidney in the realm of plot as well. For such an undertaking Belleforest, Webster's main source, is the natural starting-point. Once the deviations from the "nouel" have been made clear, it should be comparatively easy to see where the influence of Sidney comes in. Only when these two sources fail us, need we look for explanations elsewhere, explanations that will necessarily be of a more speculative nature.

It is immediately apparent that the outline and most details of the plot come from Belleforest. The major deviations are equally apparent and have been listed as follows by Mr. Lucas:

(1) The previous warnings of the brothers are added to make the wooing-scene more dramatic.

(2) The Duchess's "guilt" is discovered at the birth of the first

child, not the second. The manner—by the dropping of a horoscope—is Webster's invention.

(3) The pretended peculation of Antonio is also Webster's addition. He says nothing of the stay at Siena. And the Duchess parts from Antonio before, not after, their pursuers appear.

(4) The tortures of the Duchess, the deaths of the brothers, and the manner of Antonio's murder (*i.e.* practically all IV and V) are new.

(5) Julia and her sub-plot are added. Castruchio has become her husband, instead of a Cardinal.

(6) Bosola, instead of being simply the final assassin, becomes the villain of the whole piece.[12]

This is a correct and useful summary of the changes that obviously matter. But there are others, perhaps more easily overlooked, which must also be considered here. Thus the historical setting is, as we have seen, only partly that of Bandello and his translators. Although Belleforest without hesitation places the incidents of the story in the reign of Julius II, the Pope "who was more martiall than Christian, and loued better to shed bloud than giue blessing to the people," Webster makes his characters refer to persons and events connected with the battle of Pavia in 1525.[13] One such person, the Marquis of Pescara, is included among the dramatis personae; Silvio Savelli's little army that besieged the French garrison in the castle of Milan for a few months in 1512–13 is changed into a mighty imperial host, in which Silvio himself has only a subordinate post. Delio, by no means a soldier in Belleforest, is loosely attached to the camp, as is also Count Malateste, a suitor for the Duchess' hand.

A far more important personage in the camp is the Cardinal of Aragon, whom Webster makes commander of the army together with Pescara and Lannoy. He is introduced in the play as

a brave fellow,
Will play his five thousand crownes, at Tennis, Daunce,
Court Ladies, and one that hath fought single Combats.

(I, i, 154–156)

Reference is made to his reputation as a soldier, acquired before he was made Cardinal. At the shrine of Loreto he delivers up his ecclesiastical insignia and is dressed in steel. He joins the other warriors at Milan in the last act of the play but is never allowed to display his ability as a general.

It has already been pointed out that there is nothing in Belleforest to suggest these warlike activities. Nor are the circumstances under which the Duchess is warned of ever marrying again nor those under which her marriage is discovered similar to those in the "nouel." No warnings are issued in Belleforest, and the whole secret investigation into the Duchess' private life is directed by her brothers from Rome. They certainly never condescend to spying themselves. Both the visit of the brothers in Act I and that of Ferdinand in Act III are thus without foundation in the main source. The false key and the Duke's secret entry into his sister's chamber are apparently also additions by Webster.

The wedding ceremony is undoubtedly performed in accordance with Belleforest's indications. The clumsy "for the present time they passed the same [the marriage] in words" is correctly interpreted as signifying a marriage *per verba de praesenti,* which also duly takes place.[14] But Webster puts Cariola behind a curtain, allows her to overhear the conversation of the lovers, and produces her as a witness to the ceremony when the crucial moment comes. Wooing and wedding are thus joined inextricably together, while Belleforest allows a day to pass between the two. No details are given in the source, while a ring and mutual vows play an important part in the play.

The last of Webster's deviations from Belleforest that need occupy us here has been generally neglected, although it is by no means unimportant. In the play the Duchess is twice told by Ferdinand that her offences have been pardoned, the last time as a preliminary to the kissing of the dead man's hand and the discovery of the wax figures. What seems to be a reconciliation is really cruel revenge. This is a refinement of which Belleforest is innocent. It is one of the details in *The Duchess of Malfi* of which the main source gives no explanation. If we persist in considering one desirable—and it is our duty here to persist—we must search for it elsewhere.

The Significance of Arcadia

If we look for the origin of the pardon promised to the Duchess in the other accepted source of the play, Sidney's *Arcadia,* we shall also look in vain. This should be noted, for the episode occurs in a scene where Sidney's influence is very marked. In Belleforest–Painter the Duchess is not brought "by degrees to mortification," she is left alone with her children until she is strangled "certayne dayes after hir imprisonment." [15] In *Arcadia* more ingenious methods are resorted to, and these seem to have left their mark in *The Duchess of Malfi*. The situation in the prison, with Ferdinand intently watching his sister's reactions to his experiments in mental torture, was probably modeled on Queen Cecropia's behavior to Pamela and Philoclea, a theory confirmed by several verbal echoes from Sidney in this part of the play. Fanciful though it may appear, Webster's villain-prince was probably taught a lesson in cruelty by Sidney's villain-queen.

The conduct of the young princesses cannot, however, be considered a satisfactory source of inspiration for Webster's presentation of the Duchess in prison, their attitude to life and death being highly emotional at this point. But in Queen Erona, another princess in distress, Sidney provided Webster with a better model. Her behavior clearly suited the dramatist's intentions admirably, for not only was his heroine made to conduct herself in the same way, but the very phrases in which Erona's reactions are described were transferred almost word for word into the play. One of the significant stages in the development of the Duchess from Belleforest's arrant sinner to the innocent martyr she appears in Webster's Act IV seems to have been Sidney's Queen Erona.

Episodes in *Arcadia* are thus partly responsible for the conduct of both villain and victim in the torture scenes, as sources of inspiration and points of comparison. Important details have the same probable origin. The darkness and the shrieks and capers of madmen with which the Duchess is plagued were suggested rather by the "terrors, sometimes with noices of horror, sometimes with suddaine frightings in the night," with which the Arcadian sisters are visited, than by Belleforest's reference in passing to "Mad and Bedlem persons." [16] Suggested, but no more. Webster's elaboration of the "noices of horror" has no counterpart in Sidney. Nor can anything faintly similar to the kissing of the dead man's hand be found there.

The introduction of the wax figures of Antonio and the children, which is part of Ferdinand's scheme for the torturing of his sister beyond endurance, has, however, a well-known Arcadian parallel in the mock executions of Pamela and Philoclea. In both works devices are used to make an imprisoned lady believe in the death of someone who is actually still alive. The intention is the same, the setting the same. Pamela resolves to starve herself to death, the Duchess threatens to do the same. But in Sidney we are faced with two incidents, separately treated although part of the same plan, laboriously and awkwardly staged, while in Webster we have a swift dramatic discovery at the drawing of a curtain. Whether the differences are striking enough to make a search for an additional source advisable is a question that will be put in due course. Suffice it to say here that the idea of the counterfeit bodies was probably suggested to Webster by the mock executions in *Arcadia*.[17]

Another episode that Webster seems to owe to Sidney is that of the echo scene, if only because his familiarity with *Arcadia* is proved, while his knowledge of the various plays in which similar

scenes occur is only conjectural. The melancholy of the Websterian scene may point to one play, its comparative lack of
artificiality to another; neither quality is very marked in Sidney's
eclogue. Having no way of determining how the echo scene was
actually suggested to Webster, we could, however, do worse than
assume an Arcadian origin, perhaps with some allowance for the
simplifying influence of a possible dramatic tradition.

Webster's debt to Sidney, then, is considerable, but at the same
time curiously limited. An episode in *Arcadia* suggested a scene
in *The Duchess of Malfi,* another episode suggested another
scene, a few phrases finding their way into the play almost word
for word, but in the elaboration of these scenes Webster deviated
so immediately and radically from his original that, without the
indubitable verbal echoes, it would be far from easy to recognize
the extent of his indebtedness.

A debt of ideas for dramatic action rather than patterns of
action—this nature of Webster's dependence on Sidney makes it
tempting to look for the origin of the fate that overtakes Bosola
and the Aragonian brothers in the destruction of the wicked
Cecropia and her son. It may be argued that the repentance of a
villain and the vicissitudes of chance are devices readily resorted
to by Elizabethan dramatists when they wish to dispatch two
villains at one stroke, Sidney's Amphialus being furthermore
hardly a villain at all. This is true, and I do not wish to labor the
point. It is perhaps of some interest, however, that although
Webster could find no precedent in Belleforest for the final scene
of his play, Sidney furnished him with an excellent example of
justice overtaking malefactors.

Problems and Solutions

The Warlike Cardinal: History and Bandello. Although several
of Webster's notable deviations from Belleforest can be explained
with references to *Arcadia,* a number of similar problems remain
to account for. The nature of the present inquiry will make it

necessary to search for explanations in "potential sources" before other possibilities are tested. However, the versions described in Chapter I have all so much in common with *The Duchess of Malfi* that a serious consideration of their relationship to the play must now claim our attention.

Some of Webster's most startling additions to Belleforest's story concern the figure of his master villain. The strange fact is that Webster's Cardinal seems in one important respect to be drawn from the historical Lodovico d'Aragona rather than from any literary model. Here was a dignitary who had fought single combats in his youth, had served as an officer against the French while still in his early twenties and taken joint command of an army in 1510, on which occasion it is known that he was dressed in armor. This is surprisingly close to Webster's version, so close indeed that it does not seem warranted to write off the parallels as pure coincidence. And the mystery deepens when it is remembered that, although neither Bandello nor Belleforest mentions it, the Cardinal and his brother paid their sister a visit on a pilgrimage to Amalfi in August 1509, only a year before her flight to Ancona.[18] The awkward fact is, however, that there is no safe evidence at all to suggest that Webster knew the true history of his characters. His distortions of the historical setting and the almost complete lack of contemporary references to the Duchess' tragic end make such knowledge very unlikely. Nor can it be assumed that the fame of the Cardinal of Aragon, although not inconsiderable in his day, was sufficiently great and widespread to reach the ears of an English dramatist writing a century after the event. An explanation must reluctantly be sought elsewhere.

It is obviously not to be found in the story told by the Corona brothers. Even if it could be shown that copies of this manuscript account were much more widely circulated in late sixteenth-century Italy than their present scarcity outside Naples indicates, their story would have very little bearing on our argument. The only significant information it adds to Bandello is the identifica-

tion of Cardinal Lodovico with the Aragonian brother of particularly violent habits, but this is unfortunately done with the
same obscure phrase as in the novella. The "Neapolitan oral
tradition," possibly represented in *La verità svelata* by this version
and the *Vita della principessa di Francavilla,* has nothing to do
with Webster's Cardinal or with any other aspect of *The Duchess
of Malfi.*

A plausible explanation of the Cardinal's characteristics seems
instead to emerge if Bandello's "sapete come un di loro sa menar
le mani" is accepted as the igniting spark, the phrase that set
Webster's mind working in a definite direction. Material for the
filling in of suitable details could have been suggested to him
from various sources, among them Guicciardini's Italian history.
The Cardinal of San Severino, "armed withall from toppe to toe
with glittering armes," had led the French attack at Ravenna, and
Cesare Borgia himself had been a cardinal. As such he had also
appeared in *The Devil's Charter,* a play that might still be vividly
remembered by Webster and his audience.

The dramatist's knowledge of two such historical characters
may have contributed to his decision to let his Cardinal turn
general. A better model was available, however, and not only in
Guicciardini. In his version of Bandello's story Belleforest includes a vigorous condemnation of Julius II, the pope whose
warlike character and active soldiering made him a butt for
violent anti-Catholic attacks from the days of Luther and Erasmus
throughout the sixteenth century. Julius II leaving Rome at the
head of his army, Julius II in armor reviewing his soldiers,
Julius II boasting of his conquests before a shocked St. Peter—the
pope to whom Belleforest's outburst refers was as much a part of
the legend of the Whore of Babylon as ever Cesare Borgia, and
little imagination was needed to make his servants men of similar
predilections.

This explanation of the warlike nature of Webster's Cardinal
covers the facts reasonably well and does not necessitate any

extravagant claims for remarkable historical knowledge on the part of the dramatist. The passage from Bandello is, however, not an integral component of the theory, since Webster might easily have transferred the characteristics of Julius II to the Cardinal without any knowledge of Bandello's Italian text. Such a process is in fact far from unlikely. The meaning of the "menar le mani" sentence is so ambiguous that, even if strong evidence can be adduced that Webster knew Bandello in the original, very little should be made of it. But this reservation does not matter. The important fact is that, with or without Bandello, we have arrived at a satisfactory explanation of the military qualities of Webster's Cardinal. That the demands of the theater and the dramatist's recognition of them explain the early appearance of the Aragonian brothers and their active participation in the murders better than Webster's assumed knowledge of the visit of the brothers to Amalfi, goes without saying.

What other use Webster made of historical material not found in Belleforest is of little significance and seems easily accounted for. As his familiarity with the *Admirable and Memorable Histories* has already been established, it can be plausibly concluded that Goulart was responsible also for the introduction of Pescara into the play and thus in part for the transfer of the latter half of the action from 1510–1513 to 1525–1526. If, as seems increasingly likely, the author of *The Duchess of Malfi* also had Guicciardini's Italian history available, a look at his description of Pescara's great victory at Pavia would have furnished him with the name of Lannoy, Viceroy of Naples, to whom Francis I surrendered. A somewhat complex connection between the events of the play and well-known events of history might thus have been achieved.[19]

The Sudden Wedding: Bandello and Cinthio. Several incidents in the play still need elucidation. The wedding ceremony, the discovery of the marriage, the departure of Antonio, his death, and the final massacre in the dark—these are episodes which contain conspicuous deviations from the Belleforest-cum-Sidney version, deviations to which convincing parallels may be found in the other works under discussion.

The inclusion of the wedding ceremony may seem astonishing at first. Certainly the procedure as described by Belleforest ought to have been sufficient for Webster. It should be noted, however, that the interval of a day between wooing and wedding does not exist in Bandello, where the chambermaid is called in to witness the ceremony as soon as the couple have made up their minds, after talking the matter over "assai lungamente." Still more to the point is the corresponding episode in Cinthio:

> Chiamata a sè Tamaila sua balia, e una non meno amorevole che fidata cameriera, invocata la deità di quegli Iddii che i Persi pensano che a' matrimoni soprastiano, dato ad Oronte un preciosissimo anello, in presenza delle due donne si fe' sposare; e mandatele poscia fuori della camera, dopo mille amorosi baci se n'andarono al letto.[20]

There certainly exists no version of the Duchess' story in which the swiftness of the action and the significant details suggest Webster's treatment of the subject so well as does this episode in Cinthio. It provides an attractive theory: to Belleforest's slow-moving, badly managed wooing scene were added tension, color, and interesting details, and for these additions his knowledge of the novella about Orbecche was largely responsible. But a theory should be safe rather than attractive. As evidence that Webster knew Cinthio's work the episode will not do. The invocation of God and the gift of a ring are elements common to most marriages, details easily "invented" by a dramatist and as easily added to a scene such as the one in Belleforest without the assumption of any literary influence. Nor would a dramatist need special inspiration to let his lovers proceed immediately from wooing to wedding. Such a condensation would be no more than natural. Thus neither Bandello's nor Cinthio's version of the marriage is necessary for the understanding of the changes made by the

author in his transformation of Belleforest's wooing-wedding
episode into that of the play. Bandello's influence on Webster,
which could not be settled by an analysis of the case of the
Cardinal, still remains uncertain. On Webster's debt to Cinthio—
a possibility tentatively introduced here—no judgment can be
passed until the evidence is complete.

The Revenge: Herodotus, Cinthio, and Lope de Vega. But
where should such evidence be sought? Parallels between *The
Duchess of Malfi* and the Orbecche novella can easily be produced
in great number, so closely do the two stories coincide. Ferdinand
steals upon his sister in her chamber, all but surprising her with
Antonio—is this a reminiscence of the secret passage that Sulmone uses to communicate with his daughter in private? Or
should the possibility be rejected and the suggestion advanced
that Webster relied solely upon his inventiveness as a professional
dramatist when he wrote the scene? Common sense demands
that the latter course should be taken, particularly as the secret
passage plays no part in the discovery of the lovers. If a case is
to be made for Webster's knowledge of Cinthio, it should not
rest on such questionable details.

But the crucial test remains. Has the catastrophe in the novella
any sufficiently close connections with the last two acts of *The
Duchess of Malfi* to justify its inclusion among the sources of the
play? It has been demonstrated that Belleforest's version does not
provide a satisfactory explanation at this point, and that the
Erona and Cecropia-Amphialus episodes in *Arcadia* probably
suggested the behavior of both the Duchess and Ferdinand in the
prison scenes, as well as the peculiar nature of some of the tortures
resorted to. But even though I have made the most of Sidney's
influence, deviations remain that have not been accounted for.
One of them, Ferdinand's presentation of the dead man's hand
to his sister, should obviously be explained as derived from Herodotus, either in Bandello's Italian or B. R.'s English version, and

requires no further attention now. The point is, however, of minor importance. A second look at the end of the Orbecche novella may prove more rewarding.

Sulmone twice assures his daughter that her marriage is an offense that is forgiven, but only in order to make his ultimate revenge more difficult for her to bear. As a sign of complete reconciliation he even offers her a precious gift, whereupon he leads her by the hand to the room where the head of her husband and the bodies of her children are displayed. The remarkable stoicism with which Orbecche receives her father's gift should be noted, as should the groan with which one of the boys returns to life for a brief moment.

How similar this version is to Webster's prison scenes need hardly be pointed out. The whole episode is in fact considerably closer to his variations on the theme than are the elaborate devices used by Sidney, even though there is nothing counterfeit about Cinthio's bodies. The pardon and the groan, not found anywhere in the recognized sources, might raise the suspicion that Webster had read the novella; since these details are grouped around a spectacular display of corpses, the conclusion appears plausible, and since Cinthio's management of the secret wedding offers equally striking similarities to Webster's, it becomes the natural one.[21] So many parallels can scarcely be accidental. In spite of the skepticism with which we have treated the theory that Webster knew *Orbecche,* it offers the simplest explanation of some of his most notable deviations from Belleforest.

This would seem to dispose of the possibility that Webster had access to Bandello in the original, since no safe connections have been established between the Italian version and *The Duchess of Malfi.* But there is another factor to be taken into account. Webster certainly appears to have known Herodotus' tale of King Rampsinitus and the thief, and as this occurs in the novella immediately preceding *Il signor Antonio Bologna sposa la duchessa d'Amalfi,* it stands to reason that he knew both stories as they are told in Bandello. A picture of his literary background begins to emerge which indicates that the pretensions expressed in the preface to *The White Devil* were not all show.

The evidence produced on the question of Webster's debt to Lope de Vega is contradictory. There are parallels between the two plays which cannot be explained by reference to Bandello and Belleforest: Antonio's appearance in the palace of his supposedly reconciled enemy, his and the children's death, faked in Webster but real in Lope, the entry of the Duchess and the display of the bodies. But all these episodes occur also in Cinthio and have thus now been accounted for: Lope and Webster used the same secondary source. Where the Spanish dramatist deviates from both Bandello and Cinthio, notably in his version of the Duchess' death, Webster does not follow his example.

There is only one exception to this, and it concerns Antonio's departure from Amalfi. In both plays the departure is made to appear the result of his having fallen into disgrace with the Duchess, in Lope because of fornication, in Webster because of peculation. In spite of the different accusations, Webster's use of subterfuge clearly resembles Lope's, particularly as both dramatists stage the dismissal before the whole household of the Duchess. The parallel may be as good as any that can be found in Sidney or Cinthio, but isolated as it is, its significance is negligible.

For the "Cubrete" episode does not change the picture. Since Webster's tragedy was not published until 1623, five years later than Lope's, it would be possible to regard the Duchess' half-hearted attempt to adopt the old privilege of the French nobility at her court as an interpolation of the same kind as the "Concini speech" is supposed to be, made for a revival in, say, 1618.[22] But a Spanish source of the incident is most unlikely. Not only was Concini himself notorious for having appeared covered in the royal presence, but the specific reference to the custom in Montaigne's essay, which is definitely the most likely source for the episode in *The Duchess of Malfi,* makes it unnecessary to resort to the interpolation theory at all. As I see it, the passage was introduced by Webster without any knowledge of *El Mayordomo de la Duquesa de Amalfi* and was part of his play from the very first, as may also have been the case with the "Concini speech." This explanation will hold good even if Lope's tragedy should have been circulated in manuscript or if the details of its plot had been matters of common knowledge.

The rejection of Lope de Vega as a source of Webster's brings to a close the analysis of the documents in the case of the Duchess of Amalfi. It only remains to sum up my conclusions. There can be no doubt that Webster relied mainly on Belleforest's *The infortunate marriage of a Gentleman, called Antonio Bologna* for the outlines and details of his story. Various additional information was derived from Sidney, Bandello, Goulart, and Cinthio, and—probably, and far from consistently—Guicciardini's *History of Italy.*[23]

IV ❈ *The Nature of the Material*

Incidents and Intrigue

To conclude that Webster did not know Lope de Vega's *El Mayordomo de la Duquesa de Amalfi* when he wrote *The Duchess of Malfi,* and to establish safe connections between his play and Goulart's *Admirable and Memorable Histories* is to lay little claim to originality. The inference that the dramatist consulted both Bandello's Italian original and Belleforest's translation was perhaps also to be expected. The theory has been tentatively advanced before, and the circumstance that Webster probably had access to the story of King Rampsinitus and the thief in Bandello's version gives it sufficient support. The contribution of the present investigation appears to consist of a plea for the recognition of Cinthio's novella *Oronte allevato in basso stato* as one of Webster's sources and a claim for a somewhat more extensive knowledge of Italian sixteenth-century history on Webster's part than has usually been granted.

This is of course not quite all. Two potential sources, Beard and Riche, have here been silently rejected because there are no similarities between their versions and *The Duchess of Malfi* that cannot be better explained by reference to some other document. The two works that an almost unanimous critical opinion has long regarded as Webster's main sources, *The Palace of Pleasure* and *Arcadia,* have been scrutinized and a tentative evaluation of their significance undertaken. But no effort has been made to consider them primarily as material for a dramatist. In the discussion of stories and motifs that follows, attention focuses on this particular aspect. What was the nature and scope of Webster's dramatic material?

The obvious starting point is again Belleforest's "nouel," a product whose blemishes have always been much easier to detect than its merits. The latter are, however, by no means to be disregarded from the special point of view adopted here. Belleforest's ambivalence of attitude may have been disturbing to the accomplished reader's sense of artistic propriety, but it may also have been intriguing. At any given moment his characters are either good or bad; the very roughness of his sketches of such minor figures as Delio, Bosola, and the Cardinal made of them excellent dramatic material. There are, after all, comparatively narrow limits to the subtlety of characterization that can be put across on the stage, and to have a black-and-white statement of the extreme possibilities is more valuable to a dramatist thinking in moral terms than being confronted with the products of smooth impartiality.

More important figures naturally present more intricate problems, but here the great length and at times great vehemence with which Belleforest made Antonio, the Duchess, her younger brother, and the chambermaid express themselves was a decisive asset. Webster could accept or reject the words and tenor of their speeches as he saw fit, but they could hardly have failed to make an impression. In this respect the main source of *The Duchess of Malfi* could obviously be immediately useful.

But these are relatively minor matters. The essential question was naturally that of structure—the inherent possibilities of the story itself. Between the interminable speeches and the blatant moralizings it related a simple sequence of events, one that would apparently need very little pruning if turned into a tragedy. It had a central theme, it had a conflict of interests, a natural beginning, and a natural ending, if hardly of the edifying kind. Although a play based on a faithful retelling of Belleforest would not be *The Duchess of Malfi* as we know it, a tentative reconstruction of its main characteristics—even if somewhat influenced by our knowledge of the finished product—must have a direct bearing on the present argument. It will illustrate the nature and extent of Webster's problems tersely in dramatic terms and thus answer the question of the extent to which the material ever offered any valid alternative to his solution. That its preoccupation with one central issue was something very close to the dramatist's heart, however, need not be disputed.

Act I of this hypothetical play would naturally be concerned with the introduction and grouping of the main characters and the clarification of the Duchess' situation. Here the dramatist had excellent material to fall back on; vivid pictures of the Aragonian brothers could be given, definitely at this early stage rather than as late as the source indicated, and the mutual attraction between the Duchess and Antonio could be exemplified. After the possibilities inherent in the situation had been thus intimated, the act could close in the uncertain atmosphere created by threats and promises, hopes and fears.

Perhaps it would be desirable to include the proposal and secret wedding in the first act in order to avoid an awkward break in the time sequence in the middle of the second, but otherwise this episode would naturally constitute the central theme of Act II. Another scene would be concerned with the happy married life of the lovers, preferably containing at least a reference to the birth of their first child, and one or two scenes with the suspicions and investigations of the Aragonian brothers, all arranged so that the schemes and counterschemes, measures and countermeasures would create a modicum of dramatic tension.

This would reserve the birth of the second child for Act III, together with the discovery of the fatal secret, Antonio's alarm and departure from Amalfi, and the Duchess' decision to join him. Some simplification of their flight from Amalfi to Ancona, to Siena and toward Venice is called for, otherwise this act of our hypothetical play would become insufferably repetitive. The same consideration would rule out anything beyond a bare reference to the birth of the third child. If the need arose, however, the capture of the Duchess, her children, and chambermaid could also be included.

But as this would leave only the imprisonment and murders at Amalfi for Act IV and only the vacillation and death of Antonio for Act V, the choice would be most unlikely. Webster would in fact have quite the opposite problem on his hands: how to bring his tragedy to a satisfactory conclusion. No matter how he stretched his material—a dramatic escape by Antonio, an elaborately staged capture of the Duchess, at least three murders lovingly dwelt upon—it was really not solid enough to cover his last two acts appropriately. In marked contrast to what was offered in *The White Devil*, these solutions would remain very thin.[1]

And this does not apply to the last two acts alone. Any play relying for its plot on nothing but Belleforest would be decidedly tenuous. Belleforest's treatment did not present a valid alternative to Webster: the apparently promising story of the Duchess is much too simple to make a straightforward Elizabethan dramatization of it feasible. It is not sufficiently detailed, nor sufficiently complex; its very real conflict of wills finds no immediate expression in action. Faced with the problems created by Bandello's story Lope de Vega had to supply additional intrigue from the vast resources of the Spanish theater and a satisfactory ending which he found in a novella by Cinthio. Webster's situation was basically the same: if he wanted to follow the outlines of Belleforest's narrative—and we know from the finished play that he did—there was room for new material that would not interfere with the essence of the story.

Such brief accounts of the Duchess' life as Simon Goulart's, however, could be of little help to him, nor could anything of much use be derived from Bandello. Apart from a few names of insignificant Milanese characters there are only two points on which Bandello is more explicit than his translator: he makes a cryptic reference to the Cardinal's warlike nature, virtually impossible for an Elizabethan dramatist to understand, and gives a much more specific and unmistakable picture of a marriage *per verba de praesenti* than does Belleforest. In Bandello events happen fast and with considerable dramatic impact; Webster need only have followed the Italian text and a quite effective wooing and wedding scene would have resulted.

But his knowledge of Cinthio's novella supplied him with an even better description, that of Orbecche's and Oronte's secret wedding, still more detailed and to the point, and with conspicuous stress laid both on the ring that Oronte accepts from his beloved and their exchange of vows. There was no lack of material for one of the necessarily most significant scenes of the play, should Webster want to use it.

This fortunate situation was, however, unique and accidental; the important question was whether the material provided by Cinthio could add much where additions were sorely needed. The hidden passage that gave Sulmone access to his daughter's room may have suggested a method of bringing about the discovery of the Duchess' secret—thus creating complications in an act that could undoubtedly do with some suspense, even if only of a transient nature. But the problems of the last two acts remained. Although Cinthio had nothing to contribute to the incidents leading to Antonio's death, the strangling of Oronte being described without any details that even faintly recall Belleforest's story, the case of Orbecche was different. What happened to her could easily be modified to suit the demands of a play about the Duchess of Amalfi, and the modifications would change the structure of Act IV considerably. The following fusion of the two stories had much to recommend itself.

Belleforest's version of the Duchess' death has pathos but no tension. If Webster wanted to improve on this, her imprisonment could be broken by a promise of reconciliation and the handing over of a symbolic gift—and her hopes the more effectively crushed afterwards. This sophistication of mental torture could be taken from Cinthio and added smoothly and naturally to the original material. The stories are not perfectly parallel: in Cinthio Oronte and the children have already been killed when the feigned reconciliation takes place, whereas Antonio and his children remain alive at the corresponding stage of Belleforest's account. The imprisoned Duchess is, however, necessarily unaware of what has happened to her husband and eldest son, having been separated from them on the flight from Siena. This peculiar situation, which is virtually identical with that in which Orbecche finds herself, would have offered an excellent opportunity for a dramatic twist of which Cinthio, in spite of his advanced horror technique, does not avail himself. Although the bodies of Antonio and the children could not be displayed to the Duchess in the manner of *Orbecche,* she could be subjected to the same torture by being shown realistic representations of them. Thus one of the major devices by which Webster's heroine is "plagu'd in Art" may perhaps have found its place in *The Duchess of Malfi.*

Even if this should be so, the basic idea of submitting the Duchess to mental torture was probably suggested by *Arcadia,* as was the deception involved in the process. Sidney's horror devices may be elaborate and inept in comparison with the forceful directness of Sulmone's revenge and the trick of the dead man's hand adopted from Herodotus, but they are equally present behind Webster's protracted prison scenes. As was bound to happen once in a while to a writer who worked with several sources, Webster found himself with abundant dramatic material, even more than he had found for the wooing scene. Combined with the pathetic description of the death of the Duchess, her children, and chambermaid that Belleforest provided, Cinthio's and Sidney's horror effects could be worked into a satisfactorily tense and unified fourth act, with more than its measure of gruesome thrills. There was also the reference in Belleforest to "Mad and Bedlem persons," perhaps in itself all that an imitative dramatist with a sense of the grotesque needed in order to include one of the popular dances of lunatics among his "frightings in the night." [2]

Both the wooing and the prison episode, then, could be easily elaborated into major scenes of considerable complexity, quite different from their humble origins in Belleforest. Patterns of tension could be created, within an individual scene or at the most within a whole act, such as were only with great difficulty to be extracted from other episodes in the sources. Two crucial sequences in *The Duchess of Malfi* may thus have been suggested to Webster by the nature of his secondary material.

In general, however, the sources were not so accommodating. Although Webster had three largely parallel stories to fall back on for *The Duchess of Malfi,* the most important of which was available to him in at least three slightly different versions, this affluence would normally lead only to unprofitable duplication of information, without addition of incident and intrigue. For apart from the Musidorus-Pamela-Cecropia story and to some extent the Erona episode, the many interwoven narratives of *Arcadia* seem to have interested Webster very little. Arcadian, or standard Elizabethan, complications of even minor situations would evidently have interfered with his idea of a dramatization of Belleforest's story and turned his *Duchess of Malfi* into a markedly different play. Under such circumstances almost any tragedy based directly on Webster's combination of sources would be as uneventful as a pure "Belleforest play" and its plot as uncomplicated. Moreover, although what amounted to most of a presumptive fourth act could be found in the secondary material, the questionable balance of the original story was not to be remedied and a conflict of evenly matched forces was not supplied; from beginning to end the outcome of the intrigue remained almost a foregone conclusion. And, what seems equally disturbing, a final, dramatically effective and dramatically necessary, settlement of the moral issues was still lacking. On this vital point Bandello and Belleforest had nothing to contribute, Cinthio's succinct version of Orbecche's revenge was only an idea for possible further development, and Sidney's account of the horrible ends of Cecropia and Amphialus only another. All things considered, Webster's supplementary dramatic material was far from promising.

The Moral Implications

It is of course impossible to tell how determined were Webster's efforts to discover episodes that could be of use in *The Duchess of Malfi,* and to what extent materials known to him became attached to his subject by force of association. It has long been known that he borrowed shamelessly from authors of the most varying quality, from Whetstone and Guazzo, Alexander and Shakespeare, above all from Montaigne and Sidney.[3] He obviously kept a notebook in which the phrases that impressed him were jotted down and stored away for future use. Nor is this all. Promising episodes could be similarly collected; Goulart's description of lycanthropy and Herodotus' story of King Rampsinitus and the thief proved as useful in *The Duchess of Malfi* as Erasmus' friars and Bignon's conclave description had done in *The White Devil.*[4] Such selection of material may suggest a certain capriciousness which tallies well with the perhaps still prevalent picture of the Elizabethan dramatists as slovenly fellows with a cavalier attitude toward their medium and subject matter.

But what we now know of Webster's situation when he wrote *The Duchess of Malfi* is, I believe, sufficient to put him in a different category. His use of parallel versions of the basic story is remarkable. Not only could he compare Belleforest's account with Bandello's original, but he was acquainted with Goulart's opinionated version as well as with Cinthio's Orbecche novella with its detailed treatment of a theme virtually identical with that of his main source. Episodes in *Arcadia* provided an admirable parallel to the happiness and tribulations of the Duchess of Amalfi, even though Sidney's solutions to crucial moral problems are quite different from Bandello's and Belleforest's. No matter how close at hand this material may have been, Webster can hardly have come by all of it by chance; either he read widely or selected what was pertinent to his play with some care. In the light of our present knowledge it is even legitimate to assume that he knew Beard's *Theatre of Gods Judgements,* that trusty stand-by of preacher and dramatist alike, although no trace of its being used can be proved in *The Duchess of Malfi.*

Such wide reading or careful collection of material may not be characteristic of the dramatists as a group, but it is hardly surprising in one who had used sources of what may have been considerable obscurity in order to dramatize the story of Vittoria Accoramboni.[5] Although John Florio and other well-read Londoners may have been able to supply interested dramatists with what amounted to a veritable treasure-trove of Italian historical information, it would be dangerous to contend on the basis of such a conjecture that Webster ever had a choice of material in the case of *The White Devil.* Only two or at the most three written or oral versions of Vittoria's life, all of limited scope, can have been available to him, and although he may have gone to some trouble in order to get access to one or two of these, no search for the most promising story is indicated. To suggest, in the same way as has been done above with Beard, that he knew but rejected historians like de Fougasses and Riccoboni, is made inadvisable by the very obscurity and scarcity of the sources he used. Nothing beyond a necessarily arbitrary reading of as relevant material as possible need be assumed.

The case of *The Duchess of Malfi,* however, may be different.

None of the sources used was obscure, even though two of them were probably in Italian, and a prudent evaluation of material was thus definitely possible. The use to which additional incidents could be put was, moreover, severely limited by the nature of the basic story, which could obviously not be changed at will without losing its essential qualities. One of the important problems that Webster had to consider and solve was the distribution of praise and blame among the main characters, a question on which each new commentator on the consequences of unequal marriages naturally had some observation to make. Thus, while the comparative poverty of plot from which Belleforest–Painter's "nouel" suffers would be sufficient reason for the dramatist to go beyond it, the secondary sources contained ideas with a direct bearing on a central issue in his play.

The most cursory examination of Belleforest's narrative and Webster's tragedy reveals a radical difference in moral outlook. To paraphrase the observations of most critics who have commented on the matter, the translator and the dramatist seem to inhabit separate worlds.[6] Even though Belleforest's attitude to his subject has frequently been misunderstood, this remains a justified statement. To the rigorously moralistic Frenchman everyone involved in the Duchess' story was criminal, sinful, and to be condemned. But in spite of the highly pertinent questions it could raise, it was scarcely immediately acceptable to a Jacobean dramatist. Some moral distinction between heroes and villains was normally desirable on the stage. Every play could not be a *White Devil*.

No such distinction could be found in Bandello's novella. It was not the habit of the Bishop of Agen to voice his opinions on moral issues, no doubt particularly when it might offend influential cardinals and princes. This worldly-wise, if not cynical, attitude could not but have a certain appeal to the creator of Flamineo and Francisco de Medicis, although not even he could be expected to maintain it throughout a whole play. As a bald statement of the unpleasant consequences of a Duchess' violation of social decorum, however, Bandello's story could hardly be improved upon. It may not have presented a real alternative, but it was something that Webster could not easily have forgotten.

To what extent Beard's and Goulart's interpretations of Belleforest influenced Webster's thinking on the problems of praise and blame, sin and retribution, is of course impossible to ascertain. Very few Elizabethans seemed to be able to refrain completely from discovering the hand of God in the disasters that overtake sinners (Marcello is made to comment in this vein in *The White Devil*), but seldom can two such unattractive instruments for the punishment of lust and ambition as the Aragonian brothers have been offered to the English theater public. One of the hack writers for the stage might have fallen for such a simpleton's attitude to a moral dilemma, but not John Webster, whose treatment of the rewards of virtue and the penalties of vice in *The White Devil* is nothing if not sophisticated. The challenge of Beard and Goulart, those two merciless Christian upholders of social decorum, can hardly have given him serious pause, although some members of his audience would undoubtedly have been ready to accept it as genuine.

Cinthio's attitude to the secret marriage between a princess and a commoner is radically different from Beard's and Goulart's. Not only does he treat the lovers with indulgence, he actually makes a king deliver an impressive summary of the arguments in their defense—and this even though Orbecche is Sulmone's daughter and Oronte his subject, a situation that would have made Bandello's French and English adapters resort to language of unrestrained violence. Birth, social status, and property matter little in comparison with virtue; marriage between a princess and such an accomplished commoner as Oronte may be a sin, but it is a "peccato d'amore," an act that should be forgiven, not condemned. The laudatory comments that Whetstone, Greene, and the author of *The Forrest of Fancy* make on the marriage of the Duchess of Amalfi show that tolerance in these matters was not limited to Italian novellieri.

How an understanding but sincere Elizabethan moralist like Whetstone would have reacted to Cinthio's decisive solution of the Sulmone-Orbecche conflict remains an open question. That revenge for blood, followed by suicide, represented a real alternative in the world of the Elizabethan drama is, however, beyond doubt.[7] The problem of the rights and responsibilities of the revenger lies at the core of the revenge tradition, and Cinthio's manner of settling it had presented itself to more than one author of revenge plays. Although it was not directly applicable to the Duchess' story, it opened familiar moral vistas. The wicked could be disposed of together with the virtuous.

The relevant episodes in Sidney's *Arcadia* bring under debate problems both connected with the marriages of the great, and concerned with retribution and revenge. Although Musidorus is in the end recognized for what he is and the issue of a commoner's right to marry a princess is consequently not brought to a head, his abduction of Pamela constitutes a breach of propriety commensurable with that of which Antonio is guilty, and the matter is accordingly treated at length with all the seriousness that the author can muster. The final decision in favor of the lovers is reached only after involved legal arguments, and the whole treatment of the situation goes far to show that questions touching a princess' honor were not taken lightly.

The conclusion of Pamela's and Philoclea's tribulations at the hands of Queen Cecropia raises different questions. Not only does the fortitude and spiritual nobility of the sisters make Prince Amphialus realize the wickedness of his ways but, stricken with remorse, he turns against his mother, whose willing tool he has been so far. Her death through what looks like divine interference, followed by the suicide of her penitent son, brings the episode to a highly edifying close. Although it was scarcely possible to introduce this solution to an Arcadian dilemma into

Belleforest's story, it did represent an alternative to the desperate revenge of the outraged Orbecche and to the acceptance (laudatory or denunciatory) of the power of the Aragonian brothers to punish the Duchess at their discretion. The fact that Webster had already done some serious independent thinking on questions of sin and retribution would not make the alternative less valid.

This analysis of the different moral positions assumed in Webster's sources is not intended to suggest that he read them with the purpose of having such issues illuminated. Why he read them and how he read them is not for us to say. But in the course of his reading he could not have helped noticing that a wide variety of attitudes existed to the questions posed by the Duchess' story. Being a dramatist working for the popular stage and profoundly concerned with problems of private and public morality, he almost had to take these attitudes seriously in order to produce a successful play on the subject. The obvious fact that his solution might easily have been the same without the use of multiple sources does not affect my conclusion: the nature of Webster's dramatic material repeatedly invited him to fashion *The Duchess of Malfi* into a significant commentary on the moral issues raised by its action.

It is difficult to decide just how familiar the tragic life of the Duchess was to Webster's audience. In its essentials it was, however, immediately recognizable to most educated Englishmen, for the development of her story follows a pattern established in the Middle Ages and stoutly maintained throughout the Elizabethan period. It is represented not only by the successive editions of the *Mirror for Magistrates* but also by most translators and adapters of Italian *novelle*. "A noble lady marries a commoner against the will of her relatives and great calamaties ensue . . ." Webster's basic story, the frame on which he built his tragedy, had the makings of a moral *exemplum* in it—to judge from Beard's and Goulart's inclusion of it in their collections of edifying stories and Whetstone's and Greene's references to it, it was already regarded as one. A serious dramatic treatment of such a subject could accordingly be expected to attract considerable attention.

This was all the more so as the Duchess' behavior was far from unparalleled in Elizabethan and Jacobean England. From time to time similar cases caused great stir both at court and among the gentry. The alarm expressed was only seldom based on religious considerations, although some Elizabethan divines fondly hoped that widows would abstain from taking second husbands. Other clergymen, who probably held views too strong on the nature of womankind to suggest a life of contemplation, made it a point to recommend remarriage as soon as possible, and their advice was wholeheartedly followed, with the happy result that few prominent widows remained independent for long. The succession of husbands usually accomplished by the long-lived among Elizabethan ladies provides the best possible proof that the opinions voiced against second marriages of women went unheeded.[8]

But whether they married for the first, second, or third time, the members of the Elizabethan nobility and gentry almost invariably chose their partners from their own rank of society. They were, to be sure, not induced to do this out of respect for degree alone; property interests and political considerations were also frequently involved. We do, however, know that Frances Walsingham, Sir Philip Sidney's widow, was regarded as too far beneath the Earl of Essex in rank to be a proper match for him, and her case was by no means unique. Lady Mary Grey, being of royal blood, was obviously in a special category. When she married a sergeant porter, Elizabeth had her sequestered from her husband for life.

A further complication arose if a great lady married in secret or, even worse, against the express command of the sovereign. Under such circumstances neither Elizabeth nor James showed any compassion for suffering couples, particularly if their marriage was considered dangerous to the state. Elizabeth's treatment of Lady Catherine Grey and Lord Edward Seymour is matched by James's wrath against Lady Arabella Stuart for her union with Seymour's son. Although a secret marriage, at a private ceremony or *per verba de praesenti,* was "absolute marriage" and as such indissoluble, its consequences could be disastrous. Webster's audience hardly needed the living example of the Lady Arabella to remind them that the laws of decorum that governed the marriages of the high and mighty were not broken with impunity.

Against this background the laudatory references to the Duchess in *The Forrest of Fancy* and *Heptameron of Civill Discourses,* not to mention *The Carde of Fancie,* guarded though they are, seem curiously out of place. The "official English attitude" to the question raised by her behavior would undoubtedly have coincided with Belleforest's rather than with Cinthio's point of view. But theory is one thing, practice another. The number of cases where we know that decorum was flouted is quite impressive, particularly if it is remembered that our knowledge of contemporary reactions is largely limited to those marriages that created sizable scandals. At times harsh measures were taken, at times leniency was observed. What we definitely know is only that the subject was highly topical and that consequently the story on which Webster based his tragedy possessed great inner vitality. That is fortunately sufficient for our present purposes.

But the brief allusions to the Duchess of Amalfi in Elizabethan literature not only support this interpretation, they also point to a further possibility. Some acquaintance among the reading public with the novella of Bandello and Belleforest seems to be indicated, otherwise references to its central conflict would lose most of their meaning. What Whetstone has to say about the Cardinal is perfectly consistent with such an assumed familiarity: "this Cardinal . . . is for this Act, so often regestred for a Tirant, as I feare mee he will neuer come among ye n[u]mber of Saints." [9] Barnabe Riche's conspicuous borrowings from Painter are, as I see them, evidence that points in the same direction: the dialogues would be recognized by the attentive reader and perhaps make him turn to the original story. Thus the unfortunate Duchess of Amalfi was not unknown in England when Webster made her the heroine of his tragedy.

Under such circumstances it was inevitable that some spectators should see in *The Duchess of Malfi* a variation on a theme with which they were already familiar. They would recognize the implications of the Duchess' marriage, knowing the arguments for and against such conduct. It is also possible that a few literati would be able to follow Webster's deviations from Painter and be thrilled or shocked by his innovations and perhaps even recognize their origin. This may well have been part of the artistic intention of the dramatist who penned the pretentious preface to *The White Devil* and treated his audience to semi-quotations from Montaigne.[10]

This is not a point of major importance, nor does it necessarily apply to other contemporary dramas and dramatists. What really matters here is the familiarity of the story and the living issues that it embodied. It raised important questions and demanded well-considered answers. Because of the shortcomings of the story from the point of view of plot and incidents, the nature of the answers, moreover, would affect the structure of the finished play. Not only would an acceptable conclusion have to be supplied, but it would have to be adequately prepared for.

The different solutions to the basic moral problems that the sources suggested have been analysed and classified, some as valid alternatives, others as mere points of departure. Independent solutions would also occur to any intelligent and experienced dramatist. But we must discriminate among the possibilities and try to see them in relevant dramatic terms. Webster was, after all, a writer of considerable subtlety and skill. Since the antagonists of the Duchess were so exceptionally repulsive as the Aragonian brothers, the temptation to follow the rigorously moralistic interpretations of Beard and Goulart can hardly have been great. Not even Lope de Vega with his Spanish concept of family honor could bring himself to depicting such princes as ministers of justice.

But a toning down of these questionable characters might have offered an attractive alternative. They might be changed from the justified but bloodthirsty revengers they are in Belleforest into unwilling but dutiful upholders of propriety and degree, even perhaps into victims of grim social necessity. Under such circumstances the Duchess could have remained the headstrong voluptuary that Beard, Goulart, and at times Belleforest make her. This would have provided the play with all the dramatic conflict and clear-cut moral issues it needed.

Antonio's character would present no problem. It could obviously be built around the remarkable passivity that he demonstrates in Belleforest; he would become his wife's victim rather than her partner. This would create a sort of "Insatiate Duchess" pattern, by no means without familiar precedents in the Jacobean drama. But considering the distressingly undramatic last act that the futile activities of such an ineffective hero would lead to, another possibility would quite likely appear more tempting: Antonio might, again in harmony with the sources, be portrayed as inordinately ambitious. Whether actually in love with the Duchess or only pretending, he would then be a well-matched partner for her and a more worthy opponent for her powerful brothers. This is the only aspect of the Beard and Goulart treatment of the story that cannot have failed to appeal to the author of *The White Devil*. The parallels would be very striking.

But the active part that, in the interest of suspense and dramatic balance, should obviously be assigned to Antonio need not be that of a villain-hero. If not only Cinthio but Englishmen like Whetstone and Greene could disregard the breach of propriety that a secret marriage between a princess and a commoner entailed, then it would be possible to turn Antonio into a real protagonist,

with all the characteristics of the romantic hero with which
Belleforest occasionally graces him, but with a conventional
measure of *élan* and determination added. That it would then be
necessary to tone down the "certayne vnacquaynted lust" that
moves the Duchess, goes without saying; she would naturally
assume as much of the garb of the tragic heroine as would fit her
situation.

Antonio's motives for entering upon the affair would have to
be similarly modified, prudence thrown to the winds and love
made to dominate the picture. Some ambition would be not
altogether out of the question, but it would have to be subordinated to the undoubtedly heroic qualities of strength, bravery,
and determination. Such an Oronte-like protagonist might be
turned into a dedicated avenger of his wife's death without vio-
lating probability; incidentally, he would be a most formidable
opponent for the Aragonian brothers. The crucial last act, then,
would present the absorbing spectacle of a conflict between two
evenly matched parties, and a succession of thrilling encounters
would be achieved before both Antonio and his enemies lie
dead—as the story on one hand and a virtually inviolable dramatic
convention on the other demanded that they should.

A tragedy built along these lines would have been as attractive
to a Jacobean dramatist and his audience as the previously described villain-hero alternative. Both solutions were firmly rooted
in dramatic practice and both would have offered excellent oppor-
tunities for minor modifications and complex moral evaluations.
Macbeth and *Hamlet* are no mean examples of the inherent possibilities of the two alternatives. But there was a third choice, a
type of plot with which Webster may have felt a certain affinity.
The kind of "plague o' both your houses" attitude that is a marked
characteristic of his treatment of moral issues in *The White Devil*
might be adopted here too, although a suitable ending would
obviously have to be added.

This course of action would be comparatively easy to follow.

The dramatist would be able to stick very closely to Belleforest's story, limiting himself to the modifications made necessary by the demands of the theater. He might make the Duchess behold Antonio "with a wanton and luring eye" and act accordingly, he might present Antonio as motivated either by prudence and ambition or love and obedience, and he might make the Aragonian brothers pursue them both with the utmost rigor and cruelty. The Duchess would be strangled, unrepentant and unbowed, the inert Antonio effectively disposed of, and their murderous antagonists would triumph. All in general agreement with the original "nouel," but with the whole story covering four acts instead of five.

For naturally the Aragonian brothers would not escape scot-free. They would be brought to account in the attractive fashion of *Arcadia,* not by human revengers but by a judgment of God or some vaguer sort of nemesis. As there are two different culprits to cope with, the last act would be filled with spectacular incidents and, at the same time, bring the play to a morally satisfactory close. The simplest and crudest way of doing this would be in the manner of *The Atheist's Tragedy:* divine interference at the moment when the villain is gloating over his victory. As we can see from the last act of *The Duchess of Malfi,* this was not Webster's way. Otherwise we seem to have arrived at an alternative that covers the play as we know it tolerably well.

This should not be taken to mean that Webster felt bound to reproduce Belleforest's story faithfully, compressing it into four acts while adding modifications inspired by Sidney, Cinthio, or Goulart mainly where the lack of material was embarrassing. There were other and weightier considerations to lead him to treat his sources as he did. Naturally the differences between the relatively simple play that we have sketched and *The Duchess of Malfi* are profound—witness above all Webster's drastic expansion of Bosola's part. It is only the nature of the solution at which the dramatist seems to have arrived that has so far been indicated.

Nor must the last act of *The Duchess of Malfi* be understood to introduce Webster's version of the divine judgment alternative as an arbitrary settlement of a limited moral argument. Any serious play based on the Duchess' story had to be concerned with moral issues from the very first. They had to be repeatedly held up for consideration but did not need to be finally evaluated until the last act, when the antinomies had to be resolved and the dramatist's interpretation of his subject could emerge without equivocation. This was, I take it, the general direction in which Webster's dramatic thought traveled.

But more specific answers are wanted. It is to a detailed analysis of the moral argument of *The Duchess of Malfi* that we shall now turn. The preparations have been made in a somewhat devious manner, but the purpose behind them has been a definite and practical one: to eliminate certain otherwise feasible solutions to the problems of plot and theme as not applicable in the particular case of John Webster. It will thus be possible to keep our attempt to explore the meaning of *The Duchess of Malfi* comparatively free from digressions and extraneous arguments.

V   *A Clarification of Issues*

The Creation of Mood

The nature of Webster's dramatic material has now been illuminated, and it is perfectly clear that, although Belleforest's story is frequently followed to an astonishing extent, *The Duchess of Malfi* is far more than a simple dramatization of a novella with an acceptable moral ending attached. Nor does Webster appear to have taken pains to create a play of genuine suspense, his emphasis being only occasionally on incidents and intrigue. On the whole he has elaborated rather than complicated the story; episodes such as the Cardinal's divestiture and the echo scene are the most obvious examples of this tendency. With the heroine's death occurring in the middle of Act IV, the play's unity of plot is, in fact, rather problematic.

It has, however, often been described as possessing a remarkable unity of mood. The echo scene serves no other important purpose than to create mood, and from then on there can be no doubt about the "profound, unalterable sadness" that lies brooding over the play.[1] But the scene occurs in the middle of the last act and can hardly throw its atmosphere of hopelessness over what has happened before. The spirit in which the play opens would also seem to be a different one, with Antonio rattling away like a cynical man of the world and Bosola dropping barbed remarks about everybody around him. And then there are the butts of ridicule—Malateste, the Old Lady, and above all Castruchio.

The main reason for the presence of these characters is hardly to provide comic relief to the audience. The jokes aimed at their deficiencies are for the most part embarrassingly feeble; in spite of the occasional sly *doubles-entendres* they are not even immediately effective. Less sophisticated jokes in, say, *Volpone* or *Much Ado about Nothing* succeed where in *The Duchess of Malfi* Webster's do not. He may, however, have persisted in making bad jokes about ludicrous characters for another, at least as honorable and compelling, reason: he wanted his satire to cut deep, and satirical jokes can be most effective.

This seems to fit the picture of John Webster, the dramatic satirist; the vituperative outbursts and the attempts at bitter jocularity may be part of a satiric pattern of some importance.[2] But what is it really that is satirized in these passages? A weak-backed old man is joined in matrimony to a much-courted young woman with a limited interest in matters of the spirit—is this a satire of the prevalent *mariage de convenance* habits of James's court? The same miserable fool tires to practice the standard tricks of a successful courtier—is this a satire of the shameless office-seeking for which the same court was notorious? An old lady paints her face and is viciously blasted for it—is this a satire of the make-up habits of Jacobean court ladies? The objects of satire are all unmistakable and, no matter in which perspective they are seen, all petty and trivial. This aspect of Webster's art does not seem to succeed in *The Duchess of Malfi;* in comparison with Camillo and the other targets of Flamineo's ridicule, Castruchio and the Old Lady are mere excrescencies.

But Castruchio is integrated, if at all, with the secondary plot of the play, and this still remains to be examined. From the point of view of satire the secondary plot is singularly unrewarding. A cardinal takes a mistress, plays with her cruelly and cunningly, gets tired of her and is forced to kill her; whatever reflections on the moral turpitude of high Catholic churchmen this contains, the satire is at the most incidental, it does not contribute energy and impact to the sequence. Julia, the Cardinal's mistress, is depicted as going from bad to worse, being murdered in the midst of her inept performance as a "great woman of pleasure" and courtly *intrigante*—the possible satirization of the foibles of contemporary court ladies is indeed of the weakest kind. The main purpose of the Castruchio-Julia-Cardinal by-plot is quite simply not satiric in any but the vaguest sense of the word.

Nor does it really complicate the main intrigue of Webster's play to any appreciable extent. Nothing comes of Castruchio's two appearances and very little of Julia's association with the Cardinal, which does not affect the course of the action until the last act. What she does here is also curiously ineffective: some tension is no doubt introduced before the audience realizes what her courting of Bosola will bring with it, but then she dies, and the result of the intrigue is simply that Bosola recognizes the Cardinal as his fellow murderer. From the point of view of dramatic denouement this is an important discovery since it gives the final direction to Bosola's vacillating course, but it is certainly not brought about in the only possible manner. On the contrary, almost any way to unveil the Cardinal's villainy to Bosola would have served; the final outcome of the intrigue actually effected is out of proportion to the intrigue itself. Structurally the subsidiary plot of *The Duchess of Malfi* is of uncommonly little significance.

There may, however, be an element of considerable relevance that is discernible equally in the conduct of Julia and the ridicule leveled at her husband. That is the constant harping on sex. The incidental value of this should of course not be disregarded: like his fellow dramatists Webster knew how to present a situation based on mounting sexual tension so that the blood pressure of the audience would be agreeably stimulated. Zanche's direct method of approaching Mulinassar-Francisco in *The White Devil* is paralleled by Julia's sudden wooing of Bosola. The immediate impact of both episodes is remarkable.

But it is possible to draw a distinction between the two plays that may prove rewarding. In *The White Devil* the passion of love and lust may be looked upon by Flamineo and Francisco as degrading, unworthy of intellectually alert human beings, but it is condemned as foolish, comical and dangerous, not as tiresome and disgusting. The implication is approximately that sex is inevitable and occasionally great fun. Zanche is foolish as well as lecherous, but it is a folly to be laughed at; her behavior has a definite touch of the farcical about it. The jokes aimed at Camillo are intensely nasty, barbed, and cruelly to the point, but it is the expressions of his passion for Vittoria that are ridiculed rather than the passion itself. His ineffectual lust is furthermore contrasted with the dashing animal spirits of Brachiano and Vittoria, to whom the perfume and suppliance of a minute is an object most sweet and frantically to be pursued. Balance between, we might say, lust and lust is thus achieved, and no sweeping condemnation of man driven by sexual passion attempted.

No such balance is struck in *The Duchess of Malfi*. The intermittent and rather inane baiting of Castruchio only makes his motives and behavior more contemptible, and the exaggerated directness of Julia's conduct is harsh caricature but not farce. To judge from the evidence so far examined, sexual depravity is regarded as a very serious matter in *The Duchess of Malfi*. Since the main action of the play is based on the consequences of a deliberate flouting of the laws guarding sexual decorum, the by-plot may serve to provide a commentary in word and action on the heroine's behavior. Whether we find in what is offered a contrast or a parallel, the effect of *The Duchess of Malfi* may largely depend on the degree of relevance that this commentary achieves.[3]

But sexual depravity is only the most obvious theme to which

Webster comes back time and again in the tragedy. The comments on Malateste's character and especially Bosola's baiting of the Old Lady point to the presence of a concept of more far-reaching implications. These episodes are concerned with an aspect of human life that clearly fascinated Webster at the time: the contrast between seeming and being or, more particularly, the occurrence of evil in the disguise of beauty and truth.[4] The theme is varied many times in *The White Devil*, in whose title it is actually announced, and it is held up for consideration with remarkable insistency in the sister tragedy:

> oh, that to avoid ingratitude
> For the good deed you have done me, I must doe
> All the ill man can invent: Thus the Divell
> Candies all sinnes o'er: and what Heaven termes vild,
> That names he complementall.
>
> (I, i, 297–301)
>
> *Though Lust doe masque in nev'r so strange disguise,*
> *She's oft found witty, but is never wise.*
>
> (II, iii, 92–93)
>
> Vertue, where art thou hid? what hideous thing
> Is it, that doth ecclipze thee?
>
> (III, ii, 81–82)

In a play where one of the central characters repeatedly changes his "garb" in order to conspire and deceive, where the blackest villains are hidden in the resplendent garments of a prince and a cardinal, and where the main action hinges on the heroine's successful deception of the world, the pertinence of these observations is immediately recognizable. And there are many others of the same kind. As elaborated by Webster, Belleforest's story became an admirable vehicle for a significant running commentary on a paradoxical situation that seems to have struck the dramatist as lamentably prevalent and particularly obnoxious.

It is legitimate and sensible to argue both that Webster's preoccupation with these problems is quite exceptional and that it is a result of his acquaintance with Montaigne's Pyrrhonism, but

this does not make *The Duchess of Malfi* a play about the tragic
contrast between appearance and reality or even about the true
nature of virtue and vice.[5] The dramatist's reflections on this
aspect of life may be integrated with the story without providing
it with a major theme. Their relevance may be indirect only.
Bosola's long meditation on "this outward forme of man," in
which superficiality and deceit are regarded as at the very core
of human existence, may be a case in point:

> But in our owne flesh, though we beare diseases
> Which have their true names onely tane from beasts,
> As the most ulcerous Woolfe, and swinish Meazeall;
> And though continually we beare about us
> A rotten and dead body, we delight
> To hide it in rich tissew—all our feare,
> (Nay all our terrour) is, least our Phisition
> Should put us in the ground, to be made sweete.
>
> (II, i, 54–62)[6]

This passage is more than a condemnation of man's incorrigible
habit to deceive and betray; the emotion that it voices is disgust,
disgust with human existence per se, as a bestial existence in
which deceit and violence are inherent. Cynical resignation is
added to condemnation. What sets off this far-reaching argument, however, is curiously limited in scope: the meditation is
actually a following up of the preceding virulent attack on the
"scurvy face-physicke" of women, as exemplified by the counte-
nance of the Old Lady. The balance between cause and effect is
unsatisfactory: Webster's concern with the outward form and
inward spirit of man may be genuine and even profound, but,
to judge from this crucial passage, it may also be of a largely
incidental nature. All things considered, it would be unwise to
treat the recurrent reflections on appearance versus reality as more
than a subsidiary theme in *The Duchess of Malfi*.

This is not to underestimate the importance of the theme but
only to assign to it a different function. It seems to be in the same

category as the harping on sex: it runs through the play from beginning to end, now purely incidental, now with an immediate bearing on larger issues, but constantly doing its work to build up the atmosphere that surrounds the Duchess and Antonio—an atmosphere of lust and deception. Frequently the two themes are mixed: it is lust that masks in strange disguises. From Bosola's scolding of women, with its obvious sexual overtones, to his general denunciation of human nature is but a short step.

The elements that give a peculiar flavor to Bosola's meditation and to the running commentary as a whole, have now, I believe, been laid sufficiently bare. Although in each individual case the satire in *The Duchess of Malfi* is singularly ineffective, the constantly negative and wryly twisted outlook cannot but color most of the generalizations made. What appeared sporadic and undramatic criticism of various aspects of contemporary life now acquires a new proportion; when Webster's satire is applied to the subjects of lust and deceit, it serves the highly dramatic purpose of binding these two themes together so firmly that plausible expressions of a definite view of life emerge. The reflections that give to *The Duchess of Malfi* the characteristic unity of mood that the play possesses thus become those of a highly observant cynic, thoroughly disgusted with human existence.

It is no coincidence that this view of life is identical with that voiced by Bosola in the "garb" that he most frequently assumes. "Thys newe Iudas and pestilent manqueller" Daniel de Bozola has certainly traveled a long way. Instead of following the excellent pattern of "My lord, his throat is cut; that I did for him," thereby relegating him to the category of common cutthroats where Belleforest puts him, Webster made Bosola a key figure in *The Duchess of Malfi*. The firmly established traditions of how a tool-villain and a malcontent should behave undoubtedly contributed to the function and form which the character finally assumed, but they explain the superficial aspects only. He is the master commentator of the play—observer, philosopher, satirist and actor in one person—obviously the Flamineo, the Malevole or the Vendice of *The Duchess of Malfi*. But his attitude to human activities, be they virtuous or villainous, is notably different from that of any conceivable predecessor. Whether Bosola carves for himself or for his master, he does so without any real hope that he will profit from it. He has always been "slighted thus" and expects to be so in the future. Time and again resignation marks his speeches and comments.

To what extent the mood of Bosola's reflections settles over *The Duchess of Malfi* as a whole at an early stage, is impossible to tell without a consideration of the main conflict of the play, which remains centered on the secret marriage of the heroine. But sadness reigns long before the echo scene, even though it may not reign supreme—witness the far from happy spirit in which the wedding ceremony is performed. Whether interpolated or not, the "Concini speech" has an obvious and significant bearing on the Neapolitan society in which the Duchess moves. It is unpurged, "poysoned neere the head." The background against which she and her Antonio act their tragedy is one of lust, vice and deceit. There is also, and probably from the first, a marked note of despair.

The Central Conflict

Enter Cardinal and Ferdinand. Mood is a pervasive but volatile element. To judge from the constant references to lust and deceit of which we have spoken just now, the world in which the Duchess of Amalfi lives should be monstrously evil and depraved. Studied more closely it is, however, considerably less frightening. Compared to the figures among whom the action of *Women Beware Women* takes place, Malateste and the Old Lady, Castruchio and Julia are almost innocuous, and compared to the court in *The Revenger's Tragedy* the Duchess' entourage at Amalfi is hardly evil at all. But we have only touched upon the surface of the problem so far. Those who set evil in motion must now be examined. Enter Cardinal and Ferdinand.

The introduction is managed subtly and effectively. Immediately following Antonio's discourse on the purge at the French court, Bosola, who "Would be as leacherous, covetous, or proud, Bloody, or envious, as any man, If he had meanes to be so" (I, i, 27–29), appears with the Cardinal, who is obviously a gentleman of ample means. Their conversation is noncommittal, the Cardinal's answers are curt and evasive, but the association established is not a pleasant one: Bosola has served in the galleys "For a notorious murther, and 'twas thought The Cardinall suborn'd it" (I, i, 71–72).

Ferdinand is first encountered under less sinister circumstances, chatting informally with surrounding courtiers on the highly legitimate subjects of war, women, and horses. The conversation is occasionally ribald, which may seem indicative of his real cast of mind, but only in retrospect—as Elizabethan bawdy conversations go, this is nothing out of the ordinary. A significant glimpse of the nature of Prince Ferdinand is not provided until Antonio sketches his character:

> The Duke there? a most perverse, and turbulent Nature—
> What appears in him mirth, is meerely outside,
> If he laugh hartely, it is to laugh
> All honesty out of fashion.
>
> (I, i, 169–172)

The continuation is curiously specific and may at the time appear only tangentially relevant, being concerned with Ferdinand's activities on the judge's seat. But not only is he one who "Doombes men to death, by information"; in the hands of this strange dispenser of justice the law itself is a tool "like a fowle blacke cob-web to a Spider" (I, i, 178, 181).[7] The warning to beware of the spider's web is thus sounded clearly and ominously, as the whole seemingly inconsequential passage becomes relevant to the central conflict of the play.

The sketch of the Cardinal is more detailed and equally suggestive. The frivolous and warlike side of his nature is briefly indicated before it is dismissed as superficial: "but observe his inward Character: he is a mellancholly Churchman" (I, i, 158–159). The ambiguity of this term is soon dispelled and the unscrupulous nature of the Cardinal emerges, as his use of "Flatterers, Panders, Intelligencers, Athiests, and a thousand such politicall Monsters" (I, i, 162–163) is revealed. The evil of his mind is suggested in a truly Websterian metaphor: "The Spring in his face, is nothing but the Ingendring of Toades" (I, i, 159–160) and, in order to clinch any possible argument on the matter, the devil is said to speak in the "Oracles" that he delivers. The presentation of the Aragonian brothers is thus as clear as can be; with two such "twins in qualitie" established in power, virtue will not assert itself unaided.

The domination of the brothers and the limited independence of the Duchess is brought home to the audience in the interview between the two parties that follows. The uneven balance between them puts the question of her second marriage into its proper perspective, which gives a sinister undertone to the advice they proceed to give her. The cats are playing with the mouse, each according to his own method. The voluble Ferdinand harps upon sexual matters, constantly associating marriage with vice and foulness—"luxurious," "spotted," "ranke pasture," "your darkest actions," "those lustfull pleasures"—ending his counsel with a "smooth tale" that momentarily breaks through the Duchess' studied indifference. A crude twist is given to his warnings by the display of the dagger, but the peril inherent in the Duchess' situation is more effectively stressed by the few ominous words that the Cardinal utters. If it is realized that "this Well goes with two buckets," that the obscene comments and sinister threats are thrown at her in rapid succession, culminating jointly in the "smooth tale" and the drawn dagger, the scene acquires considerable force. The Duchess is warned, but, what is equally important, the audience is also warned. And the audience has the analyses of the nature of the Aragonian brothers in vivid memory.

In his completely unambiguous attitude to the Cardinal and his brother Webster is notably independent of his sources. He disregards the shrill voice of the moralist Goulart who sees the brothers as instruments of divine justice, he refuses to be influenced by the worldly-wise tolerance of the diplomatist Bandello who sees nothing "unnatural" in a cardinal's revenge for a stain on the family honor, and he establishes at once a point of view that Belleforest does not take until much later in the story, first at the discovery of the Duchess' marriage and then most decisively when she and her children have been murdered. Cinthio's constantly unequivocal attitude to "the cruel tyrant" Sulmone was the only possible parallel offered by the sources—and a very weak one it was. Even though it was dramatically desirable to present an unmistakable interpretation of the Aragonian brothers at this early stage, Webster did it with conspicuous success, in the teeth of recalcitrant source material and with light strokes and ingenious touches.

The Duchess and Antonio. As the opponents of the Aragonian brothers the Duchess and Antonio should logically provide a moral contrast to these evil men; they should represent "virtue," at least in a vague and general way. This is a classification that has seemed natural to most critics of *The Duchess of Malfi.* Yet, if we go to Webster's sources, only Cinthio is firmly on the side of the lovers from the very first, while Bandello refuses to commit himself, and Goulart and Belleforest see only lust and ambition as the motivating forces behind their actions. Lust in the Duchess' mind, ambition in Antonio's—the character of their relationship in Webster's play is our next consideration.

The first fact to be established is significant: the two are depicted as being captivated by each other already before the play opens. Their feelings, however, are not of the same nature. While Antonio, from the distance of a subordinate, delivers a description of the Duchess in glowing colors of admiration, the Duchess, unable to restrain her passion, decides to propose to her major-domo immediately after her brothers have delivered their warn-ings. In flagrant disagreement with Bandello and Belleforest, the only two sources that pay any attention to the problem, the motives of the lovers are not entered into; the all-important fact to be fixed in the minds of the audience is that they are devoted to each other. She loves him with her entire soul and body, he adores her sincerely but respectfully. Possible doubts about their purity of heart may only arise later.

In this fashion Webster manages to predispose the spectators in favor of the Duchess and Antonio, to create the necessary emotional response to them, but also to maintain a certain ambiguity about the moral concepts they are supposed to follow. At first these appear so blurred that only a careful study of the couple as they gradually emerge in the play can serve to bring them into focus.

First the Duchess. Antonio's verbal portrait of her provides a most specific introduction; it stresses her beauty and grace, but above all her virtue and piety:

> but in that looke,
> There speaketh so divine a continence,
> As cuts off all lascivious, and vaine hope.
> Her dayes are practis'd in such noble vertue,
> That sure her nights (nay more her very Sleepes)
> Are more in Heaven, then other Ladies Shrifts.
>
> (I, i, 202–207)

Antonio is a biased witness and his testimony conventionally exaggerated, but in this speech is given the audience's first impres-sion of the Duchess, an impression calculated by the dramatist to be highly favorable and to contain a significant measure of truth. The Duchess may not be a saint, but at least one person takes her for one.

When she herself enters to have the difficult and painful inter-view with her brothers, the original impression is radically modified. She listens with composure, answers with dignity, wit, and occasionally some indignation. Ferdinand's remarks may not be fit for a saint to hear, but then we have only Antonio's word for it that she is one. A corrective has now been introduced: the saint is also a woman of the world, a *grande dame*.

And it swiftly emerges that the Duchess is considerably more than that. She confronts her brothers with a rash but unmistakable promise, "Will you heare me? I'll never marry" (I, i, 333–334), and then proceeds to defy their threats, break her promise and marry. Her determination is expressed in a most challenging fashion:

> if all my royall kindred
> Lay in my way unto this marriage:
> I'll'd make them my low foote-steps.
>
> (I, i, 382–384)

She has some fear about what her venture will bring with it, she knows that she will find "nor path, nor friendly clewe" in the wilderness where she is going—and yet she goes. There is some deceit in this, great daring and wilfulness, and a motivating force that cannot be withstood. Antonio's saint seems now to have disappeared, the great lady of the ducal court of Amalfi is also a headstrong woman completely overwhelmed by her passion. The point from which she is viewed has indeed been shifting, and it may shift again as the play proceeds.

In the crucial wooing scene the Duchess at first addresses her major-domo with a definite indication of the social distance between them—"I sent for you, Sit downe: Take Pen and Incke, and write: are you ready" (I, i, 406–407)—but her tone of benevolent condescension does not persist for more than a few minutes, as Antonio's suggestive answers bring her to a point where she can restrain herself no longer. The transfer from the impersonal to the personal, from polite conversation to active wooing, is abrupt and dramatic. Antonio, discoursing pleasantly on the "weake delight" of being a father, is suddenly interrupted:

Fye, fie, what's all this?
One of your eyes is blood-shot, use my Ring to't,
They say 'tis very soveraigne, 'twas my wedding Ring,
And I did vow never to part with it,
But to my second husband.

(I, i, 462–466)

From here the situation develops with the force of a tempest.
The ring is put on Antonio's finger, he kneels and is raised up, a
moment's hesitation follows, whereupon they kiss and embrace,
kneel together, exchange vows and go to bed in one rapid
sequence of action. It is the Duchess that takes the initiative in
these steps, and with one exception she introduces them all with
conceits: "This goodly roofe of yours, is too low built" (I, i, 479),
"I signe your *Quietus est*" (I, i, 532), "All discord, without this
circumference, Is onely to be pittied, and not fear'd" (I, i, 537–
538), "Maid, stand apart, I now am blinde" (I, i, 564–565). These
add impact to the sequence, for they are not light-hearted conceits, nor is the scene as such frivolous. A certain pattern, a certain
ritual is followed, and when the crucial moment comes, the
Duchess' monosyllabic "Kneele" cuts through Antonio's fears and
protestations, and the ceremony *per verba de praesenti* takes place.

But no ritual in the world could have concealed the whirlwind
nature of this wooing and wedding. In her firm management of
the situation the Duchess is still a great lady but, as she is prompt-
ing Antonio along, this side of her character disappears. She is
cajoling and frank, flattering and peremptory, fearful and reck-
less, but always governed by her one dominant passion, her great
love for Antonio:

                        Sir, be confident,
What is't distracts you? This is flesh, and blood, (Sir,)
'Tis not the figure cut in Allablaster
Kneeles at my husbands tombe: Awake, awake (man)
I do here put off all vaine ceremony,
And onely doe appeare to you a yong widow
That claimes you for her husband, and like a widow,
I use but halfe a blush in't.

(I, i, 518–525)

The Duchess' wilfulness and disregard for "vaine ceremony," both in the social and the ecclesiastical sense of the word, raises a point on which we have to make up our minds—as Bandello, Belleforest, Goulart, Whetstone, and John Webster had to long ago. It is the inevitable question of moral responsibility.[8] To what extent is the Duchess to blame, not pragmatically for what follows, but morally for what she is undertaking? Does perhaps Antonio's saint stand revealed not only as a very woman but as an arrant sinner?

If she does, it must be admitted that her sense of guilt is curiously limited. She asks Ferdinand to pardon her in her last interview with him, presumably for her breach of the accepted and time-honored marriage customs of the aristocracy, but that is all. The breach may be regrettable, but it does not lie heavy on her conscience. Hers is a moral dilemma of another kind: she has had to equivocate and deceive in order to go through with her ritual that builds as fast as that of the church. But this is through the force of unnatural circumstances; she has not really left the path of virtue, only the path of "simple vertue, which was never made To seeme the thing it is not" (I, i, 513–514).[9]

The distinction between this concept and Ferdinand's idea of virtue as something that his sister's conduct has reduced to "a bare name, And no essentiall thing (III, ii, 84–85) may seem over-subtle, but it is undoubtedly upheld by the Duchess. She may at first be concerned only with "The misery of us, that are borne great!" (I, i, 507) and defend herself with references to "custom" and "reputation," that is to say play it on her brothers' level, but it is "unjust actions Should weare these masques, and curtaines; and not we" (III, ii, 191–192) and, as her misery increases, a more revolutionary note is struck:

The Birds, that live i'th field
On the wilde benefit of Nature, live
Happier then we; for they may choose their Mates,
And carroll their sweet pleasures to the Spring.

(III, v, 25–28)

Her argument, expressly stated as well as clearly implied, is unequivocal. She knows that she has broken the rules of social decorum and thereby also the principles on which the established order of human relations was supposed to rest. In contrast to the generally accepted Elizabethan opinion she seems not to recognize the divine origin of this order and can thus insist that her act does not represent a violation of virtue. Her wooing of Antonio is indeed precipitate, as the close parallel with Julia's conduct should help to bring out, but no distinction between love and lust is made in the Duchess' case. In marrying her major-domo she follows nature. This, I take it, is her defense.[10]

The implications of her stand should also be spelled out. In arguing for her position and above all in silently maintaining it against considerable odds, the Duchess achieves almost symbolic stature. She points towards the establishment of an order of love and nature which she wants to uphold against the old system of law and social custom. At least once her rebellion is stated in the form of a defiant challenge:

> ANT. That we may imitate the loving Palmes
> (Best Embleme of a peacefull marriage)
> That nev'r bore fruite devided.
> DUCH. What can the Church force more?
> ANT. That Fortune may not know an accident
> Either of joy, or sorrow, to devide
> Our fixed wishes.
> DUCH. How can the Church build faster?
> We now are man, and wife, and 'tis the Church
> That must but eccho this.

(I, i, 555–564)[11]

Apart from the ironic comment that Julia's conduct later in the play provides, Webster does not dwell on the consequences of such an order, on the impossibilities inherent in the Duchess' position, and it is not for us to do so either. It is Utopian and will always remain so. But this does not detract from the value of the argument, from the acceptability of the alternative in this individual case. For there is no doubt that in *The Duchess of Malfi* the distinction between nature and custom should not only be recognized but accepted. In loving "not wisely but too well," which is, I take it, the "fearefull madness" of which Cariola speaks, the Duchess strays from the path of "simple vertue" both as a woman and as a princess. But she strays no further. She remains true to the "essentiall thing" and becomes a touchstone of natural greatness in a world where very little is what it appears to be.

This argument has taken us far from the audience's first impressions of the Duchess. The saint described by Antonio is almost forgotten, the great lady in command of her household has receded into the background, and during a few uneasy moments the Duchess comes precariously close to being regarded as a mere voluptuary. This is as it should be. Different sides of her character are disclosed, one after the other, causing the audience to hesitate and waver between different possible reactions, until the *virtù* of the Duchess is realized as well as the quality of the motivating force behind her conduct—the spirit of woman, which may or may not be the spirit of greatness.

While the spectators may be left in doubt about the heroine's behavior, Webster takes great care to keep them informed of the dangers of her plight. They know the nature of the wilderness into which she is going better than she does herself, having watched the machinations of the Aragonian brothers at close range. They understand how inadequate her analysis of the situation is:

ANT. But for your Brothers?
DUCH. Do not thinke of them,
    All discord, without this circumference,
    Is onely to be pittied, and not fear'd:
    Yet, should they know it, time will easily
    Scatter the tempest.

                        (I, i, 535–540)

Webster keeps reminding us of this discrepancy between the true peril of the lovers and the Duchess' expressions of fear. Throughout the scene the idea of violence and death is subtly introduced into her speeches. She wishes Antonio to assist her in the preparation of her last will; she does it with a smile, and writing turns to wooing, a winding sheet into marriage sheets, but a sinister note is struck and clearly heard.

And it is heard again. "The figure cut in Allablaster Kneeles at my husbands tombe" is mentioned, Antonio's *Quietus est* is signed, their marriage is a "sacred Gordian, which let violence Never untwine" (I, i, 549–550), and the naked sword, the instrument that cut the Gordian knot, is finally referred to as lying between them. The Duchess' intention in making these observations is naturally to deny the power of violence and death over their lives, but in doing so she establishes the possibility firmly in the minds of the audience. From now on the image of death is associated with the marriage of the Duchess. Even while describing her happiness, Webster prepares us for her martyrdom. The saintly figure that Antonio saw may yet make its presence marvelously felt.

No graphic character sketch of Antonio Bologna, the Duchess' chosen mate, is given. He analyzes others without being analyzed himself. It is in fact difficult to get a tolerably unified impression of him until the wooing scene, for the part he plays as commentator clashes uncomfortably with what little is told about him. His horsemanship is excellent, his honesty is beyond doubt, and his admiration for his beloved mistress is extreme—and no more information is actually given. It is a perfunctory introduction and one that differs strikingly from the pictures given in Webster's sources. Bandello mentions horsemanship and honesty, calls him "nobile" and refers to his handsome appearance but also to his richness and valor in battle, and Belleforest is quite extravagant in his praise: "Mayster Bologna was one of the wisest and most perfect Gentlemen that the land of Naples that tyme brought forth, and for his Beauty, Proportion, Gallantnesse, Valiaunce, and good grace, without comparison." [12] Add to this the description of Oronte as "il primo cavaliere del mondo" and the exceptional qualities with which, in the best heroic tradition, Sidney's Musidorus is endowed, and it will be realized that, in spite of the negative attitude taken by Goulart and Beard, Webster's putative models for his Antonio are at least introduced as men of a more heroic stature than is the major-domo in *The Duchess of Malfi*. In the play Antonio comes before us not as an outstanding courtier and soldier, but as an honest and competent court official who also has some skill in managing horses.

This impression may be modified during the wooing scene but, significantly enough, only through the attitude of the Duchess. It is a woman desperately in love with Antonio who proclaims him "a compleat man," a verdict which the audience, with its superficial knowledge of his character, may not take at its face value. Although Webster has not committed himself definitely yet, the toning down of the "heroic" qualities of the hero is remarkable, particularly as it runs counter to the traditional Renaissance presentation of the dramatic protagonist.

Another of Webster's modifications, already referred to above, is of equal interest: he gives Antonio an opportunity to express his feelings for the Duchess before he suspects the nature of her attitude to him. In doing so he deletes completely the trait of shrewd calculation that is so noticeable in the presentation of Bandello and his successors; Antonio is only granted a moment of deliberation and then has to choose:

> Ambition (Madam) is a great mans madnes,
> That is not kept in chaines, and close-pent-roomes,
> But in faire lightsome lodgings, and is girt
> With the wild noyce of pratling visitants,
> Which makes it lunatique, beyond all cure—
> Conceive not, I am so stupid, but I ayme
> Whereto your favours tend: But he's a foole
> That (being a-cold) would thrust his hands i'th' fire
> To warme them.

(I, i, 483–491)

From this speech it would seem as if ambition cooperated with his adoration of the Duchess to overcome Antonio's fears and bring about his decision, but as the scene proceeds the presence of the "sawcy, and ambitious divell" is no longer felt: his fear is vanquished by her love and his devotion, and Antonio takes part naturally and spontaneously in the improvised wedding ceremony. Webster's modification of his hero's character also made him more sincere and unambiguously honest than he appears in Bandello and Belleforest; his Antonio is clearly a man who has "long serv'd vertue, And nev'r tane wages of her" (I, i, 504–505).

The suppression of the calculating trait in Antonio's character is not limited to Act I; it acquires wider significance as the play proceeds. It is thus not Antonio who suggests his own flight to Ancona as in Bandello and Belleforest, but the Duchess who invents a subterfuge on the spur of the moment, without giving her husband an opportunity to protest. When finally their separation comes, Webster does not refer to the purse filled with money that, according to Bandello and his adapters, Antonio does not forget to take with him, but elaborates the sad farewell scene in detail, deliberately stressing the peril in which Antonio lives and how heavily he takes it:

My heart is turnde to a heavy lumpe of lead,
With which I sound my danger: fare you well.

(III, v, 106–107)

This is compliance and not circumspection. The horoscope to which Antonio resorts and the singularly ineffective way in which he attempts to protect the Duchess' secret from the prying Bosola point in the same direction: Webster's "hero" is not a shrewd deliberator, he has become a hesitant falterer. His embarrassing *esprit d'escalier,* to use Mr. Lucas' phrase—

I would this terrible thing would come againe,
That (standing on my Guard) I might relate
My warrantable love

(III, ii, 174–176)

—is a cruel twist of which the sources are completely innocent. There are elements both in Bandello and Belleforest that "justify" the change of emphasis that Webster has brought about, but they are few and the change is so pronounced that we must conclude that the hesitant, well-meaning but almost culpably inefficient gentleman that is the Antonio of *The Duchess of Malfi* was most deliberately created by the dramatist.

The toning down of Antonio's heroic qualities, the suppression of his prudence, calculation and ambition, and the stressing of his honesty, hesitancy, inefficiency and devotion to the Duchess—all these modifications are easily discerned by anyone who takes the trouble of comparing *The Duchess of Malfi* with its sources. There is, however, a pattern in them that may provide a key to what is perhaps Antonio's main significance in the play. Webster is actually cutting him down to size; all the rough traits of his character, good and bad, are smoothed out, his qualities are all rather close to what used to be considered the human average, which he thus comes unexpectedly near to representing. Thus his inferiority to the Duchess, both in ability and in social standing, becomes conspicuous. Webster's Antonio, as I see him, is a moderately virtuous, weak commoner who marries a noble lady and who is consequently, in the fruition of domestic bliss, helplessly caught among circumstances over which an average man such as he has no control.[13]

In the fruition of domestic bliss—it should be realized that the emotional relationship between the Duchess and Antonio is expressed in terms that are anything but romantic. Not the slightest reference to the wonders of falling in love and the first months of marriage is given; this period is, as it were, taken for granted, and not a single scene is devoted to the married life of the couple until their third child has been born. When the scene comes, there is no precedent for it anywhere in the sources—its introduction at such a stage actually implies a change in the sequence of events leading to the Duchess' capture—and particular importance should be attached to what it conveys: a delightfully intimate picture of happy and contented domesticity. The lightness of touch should not make anyone forget the frankness of the presentation, for this is perfectly in keeping with the general picture of Antonio's and the Duchess' life together that Webster is drawing. From the end of Act I to the middle of Act IV the audience is repeatedly asked, even forced, to consider marriage in its most basic aspect: the begetting, bearing, and raising of children. Antonio refers to it in his ironic description of marriage in the wooing scene, and the Duchess, that "excellent Feeder of pedigrees," is brought onto the stage big with child, her labor and delivery forming the background of the next two scenes. Antonio's farewell from her outside Ancona is turned into a tableaulike family group, with the threat of the "Tiger" hanging over the children, and the Duchess' last request from Cariola is to give her "little boy Some sirrop, for his cold, and let the girle Say her prayers, ere she sleepe" (IV, ii, 207–209). The silent part played by the children in *The Duchess of Malfi* turns what was merely a tragic love story into a family tragedy, with all the additional pathos and increased scope that this implies.

This heavy stress on what is best called the natural aspect of marriage is not only in harmony with the previous analysis of the Duchess' character, it makes it possible to state more emphatically what was before intimated only in passing. The "spirit of woman," whose reign over her mistress Cariola fears, can and should be understood not only in terms of sexual infatuation or any other kind of temporary emotional involvement. At first it may imply no more—and the Duchess' breach of custom may even be considered a flagrantly reprehensible act—but as events develop it grows apace, until the "spirit of woman" becomes a true "spirit of greatness," suggestive of the preserving and regenerative forces in nature. As the wife of Antonio and the mother of his children the Duchess may, for brief and scattered moments, come to represent these forces herself.[14]

We have indeed traveled far from the doubts and misgivings of Act I, when now such a drastically affirmative interpretation of the Duchess' position can be reached and upheld. The flight from the revenge of the Aragonian brothers is, however, brought to an end in such a graphic, almost emblematic scene, with references in word and gesture to the presence of the children, that the impression of a persecution of innocents that has gained ground with the audience during Acts I and II now becomes firmly established. It would undoubtedly be fanciful to say that the predicament of the group recalls the flight of the Holy Family and the subsequent murders the Slaughter of the Innocents. It is also unnecessary. What matters is that from the middle of the play the Duchess and her family are regarded as victims, not as culprits. Thus the basic principle of life becomes associated with the virtue of innocence in the character of Webster's heroine. If the situation is viewed *sub specie aeternitatis,* it is a truly formidable opposition that the representatives of things as they are have to crush.

If, however, a shorter and more practical view is taken and moral values are disregarded as of no immediate consequence, the resources of the Duchess become gradually more pitifully inadequate. And, in accordance with a familiar Christian paradox, they become so as she herself acquires greater and greater symbolic significance. As her grandeur, influence, even her princely liberty are taken away from her, she is reduced to Antonio's level, socially and dramatically. In the capacity of a loving wife and mother she too becomes a person in the average condition of mankind, "a kind of nothing," without shelter against the malice of the surrounding world. Thus the tragedy of *The Duchess of Malfi* acquires a universal significance. It is or could easily be our tragedy. There is a voice in the play that insists on this, and it is not a reassuring one.

A Case for the Prosecution? The interpretation of the Duchess and Antonio has now been pursued far into the abstract. The implications of their words and deeds in the first three acts have been explored and the characters themselves made to stand out as emblematically as possible. In order to illuminate the nature of the basic conflict the Aragonian brothers will now be submitted to a similar treatment. What, if anything, should the Cardinal and his brother, so effectively but laconically introduced in Act I, be understood to represent?

The picture of the Cardinal remains sketchy, if not altogether obscure. He appears in four different scenes, but each time his appearance is brief and the character sparingly elaborated. He is, naturally enough, in absolute command of the situation in his tête-à-tête with Julia, and his remarks of amused and contemptuous superiority seem to indicate a completely disillusioned attitude to all presumably altruistic motives, not only of woman but also of man in general. His feathers are, however, at least momentarily ruffled in the subsequent scene where Ferdinand breaks the news of the Duchess' "shamefull act of sinne," and he actually curses his sister. His failure to maintain perfect self-control is not insignificant, for it gives the audience an intimation of the fire hidden within the Cardinal and makes his assumption of command over himself and his raving brother all the more ominous. He is the one who is able to strike from afar, to "sollicite the state of *Ancona* To have them banish'd" (III, iii, 78–79). The fact that he does this in the name of the church is not necessarily a reflection upon his religion; the conventional Cariola voices an identical attitude toward the Duchess' subterfuge pilgrimage to Loreto. But the manner in which the expulsion from Ancona is presented is decisive; equipped with sword and helmet, shield and spurs, the Cardinal is seen attending to the matter personally. This is done in a dumb show whose emblematic character is clarified not only by what has gone before but also by the comments of the pilgrims. As the situation is described here, the lovers are not pursued in the name of morality and justice; it is stark and wilful power that persecutes them and thwarts their plans.

The nature of the Cardinal's reaction to the news of his sister's conduct was obviously suggested to Webster by Belleforest's description of him as "grinding his teeth togither, chattering forth of his Spanish mosel Jack an Apes Paternoster." [15] The efficiency and secrecy with which the Cardinal pursues his plans are, however, of the dramatist's own making; it is perfectly appropriate that the real wielder of power in the play should remain impersonally in the background. There was also excellent precedent in Belleforest for the attention that Webster so determinedly focused on Ferdinand's reaction to the news from Amalfi and his subsequent behavior. Extremely violent language is used in the source: "this incarnate divelish beaste the Woman . . . Ah, false and vylde bytch . . . I wil pype ye both sutch a wofull galiard . . . sutch a bloudy bargenet . . . your whorish heate . . . the caitif whoremonger"—a series of invectives that in its preoccupation with blood and sex provided Webster with the substance of Ferdinand's outbursts. It lies in the nature of the literary media concerned that such frenzy has a far greater impact in a play than in a novel. There is, however, no denying that Webster makes the most of the uncontrolled rage of his prince. No preparation is made for it; it is quite out of proportion to the warnings and threats issued before the fact; and finally it is out of proportion to that fact itself. It is indeed understandable that incestuous love for his sister has been indicated as the compelling motive for Ferdinand's course of action.[16] Such an interpretation seems to me improbable—since the tenor of the decisive passages is almost the same in Painter as in Webster—only tangentially relevant and possibly detrimental to the effect of the pertinent scenes and the play as a whole. The sudden change from a moderately passionate, although somewhat sinister-sounding prince to an irresponsible fanatic, intent upon a revenge almost holocaustic in quality, should in all likelihood be unmotivated and go beyond the natural

bounds of a psychological portrait. Webster's presentation is undoubtedly convincing enough:

> I would have their bodies
> Burn't in a coale-pit, with the ventage stop'd,
> That their curs'd smoake might not ascend to Heaven:
> Or dippe the sheetes they lie in, in pitch or sulphure,
> Wrap them in't, and then light them like a match:
> Or else to boile their Bastard to a cullisse,
> And give't his leacherous father, to renew
> The sinne of his backe.
>
> (II, v, 87–94)

There are other moments, less directly inspired by Seneca,
when Ferdinand's desire virtually to annihilate his sister, to "fix
her in a generall ecclipse," makes him fly beyond all reason,
notably when he surprises her alone in her bedchamber. On this
occasion, however, his most extravagant threats are reserved for
her unknown lover:

> Let not the Sunne
> Shine on him, till he's dead: Let Dogs, and Monkeys
> Onely converse with him, and such dombe things
> To whom Nature denies use to sound his name.
>
> (III, ii, 120–123)

In outbursts like these Ferdinand undoubtedly tends to lose his
individuality and become an "angry tyrant" pure and simple, or—
what amounts to the same thing—an abstraction, an epitome of
brutal uncontrolled violence.[17]

But there is also a scheming side to the Duke, explored in some
detail in the scene describing his decisive second visit to Amalfi,
when his ominously quiet behavior warns Antonio that something dangerous is afoot. Ferdinand the Machiavellian is, however, hardly a success, in spite of his conventionally exaggerated
statement of reliance on his own intellectual capacity:

> He that can compasse me, and know my drifts,
> May say he hath put a girdle 'bout the world,
> And sounded all her quick-sands.
>
> (III, i, 104–106)

His vanity is also neatly punctured by Bosola's quiet "I doe not Thinke so," followed by the equally blunt "you Are your owne Chronicle too much: and grosly Flatter your selfe" (III, i, 107–112). It is a justified deflation of pretensions, for, as the subsequent scene demonstrates, Ferdinand's great plan to force a confession from his sister miscarries completely—or to be more exact, he himself fails miserably to carry it out. He departs from Amalfi having learned nothing about the identity of her husband, but leaving behind him the pointed threat of a poniard, an eloquent symbol, we might say, of his insufficiency of intellect and his reliance upon force. It is thus quite proper that Webster makes fury uncontrolled and uncontrollable dominate his personality; it is a preparation not only for the complete breakdown of his mental powers that follows, but also for the resort to absolute violence which annihilates those members of the Duchess' family that he can lay his hands on. Ferdinand can after all be said to epitomize violence, and in an even more ugly and unflattering way than was at first suspected.

Violence on the judge's seat and arbitrary power on the priest's, both representatives equally evil—the interpretation is legitimate and adds significance to the play. But its consequences should not be overlooked. It concentrates on one of the two main aspects of the central conflict, but only at the expense of the other. The question posed by the Duchess' initial breach of decorum is asked several times, but answered either inconclusively or not at all. In her bedchamber interview with Ferdinand she asks him what amounts to "Why might not I marry?" three times, and the answers returned are as irrelevant as the final "I will not see thee more." The reason for this is now obvious. Being the villains Webster made them, the Aragonian brothers cannot represent a valid moral order, they cannot even argue in its defense. The antithetic note to the Duchess' nostalgic invocation of the birds that live "on the wilde benefit of Nature" is thus never sounded. In spite of the belated warning example of Julia's "natural" conduct, there is no case for the prosecution. Instead Webster seems to confront one variety of chaos with what is perhaps only another. A consideration of the proper balance between order and justice in society is only by implication part of the argument of *The Duchess of Malfi*.[18]

The other central issue is, however, squarely faced. The Aragonian brothers may not be intentionally "depersonalized"—they are after all acting parts—but by making them so aptly complement each other, Webster impresses upon the audience the amorphous and invulnerable nature of the powers they represent vis-à-vis their opponents. In an extension of the device of the well with two buckets, one is made to act directly, the other indirectly, one is made to resort to subtlety and political influence, the other to violence and brute force. Pursued as they are by the "Tiger" of this combination, the Duchess and her family soon appear in a plight absolutely hopeless. They have nobody to strike back at, they become the people things are done to. The universally valid aspect of their position is thus still more effectively underlined.

The Significance of Bosola

Like several other characters in *The Duchess of Malfi* Bosola, the hired instrument of evil, is introduced to the audience by Antonio, but is almost immediately allowed to characterize himself.[19] It is a highly ambiguous scene. Antonio's introduction is far from flattering: it is simply lack of means that prevents the "onely Court-Gall" from indulging in every vice under the sun. His ability to do evil is confirmed by references to his sojourn in the galleys for a murder, and to a certain extent he speaks the part of a hireling who has not been paid according to what he believes to be his deserts. He has good reason to feel "slighted," although hardly in the capacity of old soldier that he assumes towards Antonio and Delio. But merit is to Bosola a curious thing, totally unconnected with ethical values; even as the nature of his service to the Cardinal is explained, he complains about the "miserable

age, where onely the reward of doing well, is the doing of it"
(I, i, 33–34). This yoking together of good and evil under the
heading of merit is at least momentarily effective: in spite of the
scathing analysis with which he introduces Bosola, Antonio closes
this sequence with another analysis, astonishingly at variance
with the first:

> 'Tis great pitty
> He should be thus neglected—I have heard
> He's very valiant: This foule mellancholly
> Will poyson all his goodnesse.
>
> (I, i, 75–78)

Bosola's melancholy may hide a preponderance of goodness or of
evil; the drastically contradictory elements of his character are
intimated, but not the way in which they are mixed. At the end
of the introductory episode the figure remains an enigma to the
audience.

Bosola's knowledge of evil should, however, not be doubted.
To him as to Antonio, the Cardinal and his brother are twins in
quality, and that quality is definitely of the devil. His reaction to
Ferdinand's gift of gold is thus swift and to the point:

> So:
> What followes? (Never raind such showres as these
> Without thunderbolts i'th taile of them;) whose throat must I cut?
> (I, i, 264–266)

The subsequent argument between these two follows a strange
pattern: Bosola rejects the money and presumably also the task as
the Duke's intelligencer; Ferdinand haughtily refuses to take back
anything that he has given, referring not only to the money but
also to the position at the Duchess' court that he has procured for
Bosola without telling him about it. According to his own argument, Bosola is then, in order to "avoid ingratitude," forced to
become Ferdinand's agent at Amalfi, knowing full well that he
may be required to do "All the ill man can invent" (I, i, 297–299).

Yet his knowledge of good is really as perfect as his knowledge of evil; he is deliberately suppressing a Christian code of ethics and substituting for it a bravo's principle of absolute loyalty to his employer—as long as it does not interfere with his own interests. He has been fooled into a bargain by Ferdinand but must nevertheless honor it, at first with the loyalty of a soldier but then, as the promise of further remuneration looms larger, with the more sinister loyalty of a professional cutthroat.[20] In neither form is it a very attractive principle, but its theoretical insufficiency takes away nothing from its practical value; loyalty probably provides the most useful working basis for effective action known to man, and in comparison with the pleasant simplifications and comfortable subterfuges it offers, the absoluteness of "Let good men, for good deeds, covet good fame" (I, i, 315) has a harsh and arid ring. Bosola's choice of position is in perfect harmony with the portrait of an expert rationalizer that Webster is painting.

The equivocation involved in the choice is made quite clear by the dramatist: the alternative of rejecting the provisorship outright, thus placing himself under no obligation at all to Ferdinand, is something that Bosola is never made to consider. He turns intelligencer, allegedly with some distaste, and, as far as the audience can judge, he pursues his task with enthusiasm and glee. The apricock trick works wonders, and while it is working Bosola watches and comments in a state of admiration at his own superior intelligence and disgust with the Duchess' womanliness. The natural antipathy that he feels towards Antonio, the "Lord of the ascendant," the successful social climber, adds zest to his investigation, and it is with absolutely no sign of remorse that he ferrets out the Duchess' secret and conveys it to her brothers. That, in his desire to tear away the "strange disguises of lust," he commits the serious blunder of misinterpreting Antonio's nervous concern, is one of the ironies of *The Duchess of Malfi* that should not pass unnoticed.

At least a couple of years separate Act III from Act II and the

Duchess has had two more children, but, says Bosola, "By whom, we may go read i'th' Starres" (III, i, 73). Even if we make every allowance for the illusion of compressed time that the theater can create, he must be called a most "uncertain" intelligencer, and the prolonged failure of his mission seems also to have produced a remarkable indifference to its final outcome, an attitude that finds a characteristic expression in his insolent braving of Ferdinand. But although indifference is indicated, a real change of heart is not. There are as yet no signs of a reluctance on Bosola's part to perform his duties as a spy. He is still able to warm to his task, even though no more nasty asides referring to the Duchess' love life make this so eminently obvious.

But is there not a change of heart intimated in this absence of sexual allusions and in the extravagant eulogy, first of Antonio and then of the Duchess, into which Bosola launches when the major-domo stands revealed as a peculator? On the Duchess' direct and rather transparent question "what doe you thinke of these?" Bosola not unexpectedly delivers himself of his considered opinion of professional courtiers, perfectly in character and not only a safe but a politic thing to do. For his suspicions have been aroused—"Strange: this is cunning"—and he is primarily "playing a hunch" when he so eloquently rises to the defense of Antonio. There is, however, also an element of sincerity in this, although he has still nothing but contempt for the major-domo as an individual. In power Antonio is Bosola's enemy, in disgrace he is his fellow. Bosola is drawing the Duchess out, but he is at the same time arguing his own case as well as Antonio's, the case of men who are "basely descended" and who "deserv'd a farre better fortune" (III, ii, 294, 299). It is his own fate and the way of the world that he is lamenting.

When the Duchess reveals her secret, Bosola has to change his tune somewhat, but the theme remains the same. What, according to his view of human existence, was impossible has now happened before his very eyes: preferment has arisen from merit. A unique precedent has, in other words, been established; " 'twould make the very *Turkes* and *Moores* Turne Christians, and serve you for this act" (III, ii, 332–333). With impeccable logic and apparent candor he assures the Duchess of his allegiance: "O the secret of my Prince, Which I will weare on th' in-side of my heart" (III, ii, 344–345).

Bosola's eloquence in this speech could certainly be taken to indicate that his attitude to the lovers has changed to one of incipient sympathy with their plight. It is, however, notable that the problem that preoccupies him is still the old one of merit and reward; it may be considered in general terms, but the only person on whose position the argument bears is the speaker himself. His summing up, given in a brief soliloquy at the end of the scene, thus becomes particularly significant, as it disposes of the ambiguities of rhetoric and neatly applies to his own all-important case the general rule at which he has now arrived:

> what rests, but I reveale
> All to my Lord? oh, this base quality
> Of Intelligencer! why, every Quality i'th' world
> Preferres but gaine, or commendation:
> Now for this act, I am certaine to be rais'd,
> "And men that paint weedes, (to the life) are prais'd.
>
> (III, ii, 374–379)

But: the scruples that he voices here are the same that he harbored when he first struck the bargain with Ferdinand, and they are overruled by two weighty considerations, also perfectly familiar but now effectively clarified with a sort of ironic juxtaposition. The simplification of issues is complete. There is the question of double trust—but Bosola owes his allegiance to Ferdinand, who is the prince whose secret he wears on the inside of his heart. Thus: down with the Duchess. There is the example of Antonio's preferment "meerely for worth"—but it is reduced to its proper proportions: "every Quality i'th' world Preferres but gaine, or commendation." Thus: down with scruples. While still adhering to his—admittedly insufficient—principle of loyalty, Bosola continues to look out for number one. The vitally pertinent point that the Duchess is defenseless, the unrelieved pity of it, is not even raised.

From this interpretation of Bosola's position it follows that his advice to the Duchess to feign a pilgrimage to Loreto, transferred from the chambermaid to him by Webster, is given in order to discredit her and acquire a firmer control over her movements, not in order to help her to escape or even to prepare her better for the ordeal that is to come. His unequivocal appearance as Ferdinand's tool in the last scene of Act III tears away all pretense, and he speaks to Antonio with the utter contempt that the social climber on his way up feels for his less fortunate fellow—it is now his turn to have the whip hand. But both here and in the following scene, where he can no longer face her in his own person, his attitude to the Duchess is more complex. He is deferential, but, as I take it, only within the limits of his instructions, and at the same time remarkably curious about his victim's behavior. "What doe you beleeve?" "Is that terrible?" "Can they pratle?"—these are questions put with two aims in mind: to taunt the Duchess into direct opposition and to make her explain her motives.[21] There is not sufficient consistency behind his words to justify the interpretation that he is deliberately molding her reaction to captivity and torture; as I see it he is only trying her out, interested in discovering what makes her function in so irrational a way, willy-nilly developing admiration for her. She—but not Antonio—has now come to represent something that deviates radically from his ideas of human conduct. A kind of principle seems to be at work whose applicability he has constantly denied and whose exact nature he cannot yet identify: against all reason it seems connected with Christian charity, and he shrinks from its representative behind a mask. The stature of the Duchess is growing apace, and it is largely through Bosola's questions and comments that the audience is made aware of it.

Bosola's recurring reflections on the discrepancy between merit and reward should thus not be considered in isolation; they are most definitely part of the argument of *The Duchess of Malfi* and very close to its heart. As was pointed out earlier, his speeches on the vanity and folly of courtiers, the vanity and frailty of women and "this outward forme of man" have a similar dramatic purpose to fulfill, even though they may be irrelevant to the situations in which they occur. By stressing and exemplifying the corruption of human life, further exemplified by the words and deeds of the Aragonian brothers, Julia and her husband, Mala-teste, and the courtiers of the Duchess, they contribute to the peculiar mood of the play and the argument behind Bosola's conduct. It is his generalizations from the cases of corruption that he has observed which provide the basis for his rejection of virtue and adoption of "loyalty" as a principle of action.

But Webster brings commentary and action together in a still subtler manner. It is in Bosola's reflections that the contrast be-tween seeming and being is most searchingly considered. He sees through appearances, the sham and pretense of social life, and so does his adversary and counterpart the Duchess. For not very dis-similar reasons they both decide to uphold appearances, to seem the thing they are not. While with Bosola this has become second nature, the Duchess does it only for a time and is then forced to act the thing she is. Whereas Bosola well realizes the bearing that Antonio's rise and fall has on his own situation, he does not discern the much more significant parallelism between his own case and that of the Duchess, until it is irreparably too late to throw off his "garb" and appear in his "owne good nature." Thus Bosola and the Duchess are tied together, not only through the devices of the intrigue but also and more cogently through the logic of Webster's dramatic thought.

VI ✿✿ *The Issues Resolved*

Death and Conversion

Horror upon Horror. So far my interpretation of *The Duchess of Malfi* has proceeded by way of individual analyses of the main characters—the Duchess and Antonio, the Aragonian brothers and Bosola—and has gradually taken us through the first three acts. The last two will now be treated, separately as befits their importance, but still as parts of the unified design which, it has been assumed, governs the play.

In Act IV two representatives of opposing forces, Ferdinand and the Duchess, finally fight their conflict out, with Bosola as an intermediate agent—acting on orders, yet as observer deeply involved. It seems to be done in a most decisive fashion: the Duchess is murdered after being subjected to prolonged mental torture. The act is of central importance, and to come to acceptable terms with it is a prerequisite for a proper understanding of the whole play.

The obstacles that bar the way are formidable. The dead man's hand, the counterfeit bodies, the noise, conversation and dance of the madmen, the coffin, cords and bell, the disguised Bosola acting first the tomb maker, then the bellman, and finally the master executioner—in short, all the torture devices used are so spectacular and lurid as to raise substantial doubts about the seriousness of Webster's artistic purpose. The question of the unified design of

The Duchess of Malfi comes to the surface in any discussion of this obviously crucial act.

To be able to trace the origin of several of these devices is not to make them less spectacular and lurid, nor do we solve interpretative problems by deciding to what extent these elements are standard Jacobean fare or quite exceptional. A certain distinction in the analysis of the prison scenes should, however, be made: wax figures and dancing madmen are clean contrary things and may have been introduced for different purposes, except the obviously common one of bringing the Duchess to absolute despair. Thus the counterfeit bodies and the dead man's hand are not only variations on a literary theme, possibly familiar to some of Webster's spectators, they also serve easily recognizable structural purposes. By proffering a hand of reconciliation with an allegedly symbolic ring upon it, Ferdinand raises the Duchess' faint hopes of "pardon" only to crush them the more effectively—a type of ironic reversal repeatedly used by Webster to create tension within individual scenes. From such a starting point the next step follows swiftly and logically: the ring identifies the dead man's hand as Antonio's, and the display of bodies proves with the seemingly necessary conclusiveness that both he and the children are dead. This—first to ruffle the Duchess' composure and then to take away what might well be the basic reason for her persevering with unbroken spirit—this is the structurally impeccable purpose behind the horrors of the first prison scene. They do their work effectively and economically and have not been elaborated out of proportion to their intrinsic importance. The observation that the choice of such devices is in questionable taste need not yet interfere with our analysis.

The appearance of the madmen in the following scene is more difficult to explain. Both source and plot demanded a detailed presentation of the death of the Duchess, and once the course of gradually breaking her spirit had been decided upon, the introduction of some new devices to accomplish this became a logically desirable solution. But no combination of logic and casual references would inevitably lead to the creation of anything like the madmen episode in *The Duchess of Malfi*. There is nothing inevitable about it; many other methods would have sufficed to test the Duchess' spirit of resistance. Why then was this particular one chosen?

To answer with a reference to several dramatic precedents is really to beg the question. "Madmen as vaudeville performers" was not a tradition that had produced automation or even convention on the Jacobean stage; the desire to achieve some sort of comic or fantastic relief was at best a contributory motive. There had to be reason behind the madness, and in *The Duchess of Malfi* there is at least one obvious and compelling reason: the introduction of the lunatics powerfully suggests the ultimate disorder to which Ferdinand hopes to reduce his sister.[1] Through their influence she will become one of their kind; the purpose behind the device is thus both functional and thematic.

The relevance of the madmen is only increased by the topsy-turvy effect that Ferdinand's scheme produces. The spirit of the Duchess is strengthened, and with rigorous, nemesislike irony the schemer is made to go mad, an example of the long-range integration of which Webster was at times capable. But the madmen episode serves a significant purpose also within the smaller unit of the torture scene. The disguised Bosola is at first mistaken for a madman by the Duchess and then spends a not inconsiderable time in each of the vividly realized parts of tomb maker, bellman, and executioner. Thus he prolongs what can safely be called the nightmarish effect of the appearance of the lunatics, until the Duchess is finally killed and the mask can be lifted from his face. The unity of the sequence is undeniable, and it ought to be the product of a desire to create something more definite than nightmarish effects.

This is also the case. The harping of the madmen on the law, sex, and doomsday, the grotesque dance that follows, the deliberate care with which Bosola proceeds, the presents from the Aragonian brothers that he forces the Duchess to contemplate, the dressing of the bride to which he refers in the bellman's song—all this combines to produce an impression of ritual gone astray, an elaborately formal preparation for death which is at the same time a cruelly ironic, belated and distorted celebration of the Duchess' wedding. This is sufficiently effective integration. It is highly unlikely that Webster's dance of madmen ever achieved a so-called charivari effect by constituting an oblique but very specific reference to the remarriage of widows.[2]

The sequence from the appearance of the lunatics to the execution of the heroine is in a sense an extended masque, with music and songs, dance and stylized motion. It is macabre, but only vaguely in the Dance of Death tradition, in spite of the references to death as the great leveler in Bosola's "box of worme-seede" speech and bellman's song. It suggests hell let loose on earth, with tortures that may have forcibly reminded the audience of the threatening horrors of eternal damnation, although hardly within a definite Christian frame of reference. The devices used may rather be said to reflect the disorder of Ferdinand's mind, the conduct of the madmen more questionably the disunity of the Duchess' world—but whether such parallels are really implied or only accidental is impossible to tell. It does not greatly matter. The firmness and subtlety of the integration of episodes and themes is beyond doubt and grows more impressive the more we study it. When such an astonishing dramatic unity is achieved, it is easy to forget the perilous effects that some of the devices used may have upon the audience.[3]

The Duchess' Part. Three of the main characters participate in the events of the prison scenes; the relationship between them is vitally important for the interpretation of the sequence. The conduct of the Duchess has so far provided most of the stimuli to which the other figures have responded; as her tragedy moves towards its climax, this conduct becomes the pivot around which everything turns.

At the end of Act III the status of the Duchess had been drastically reduced, her situation made worse and the means at her command less than what applies to the human average. Her stature is, however, not reduced; the assurance of the rightness and naturalness of her course gives her an inherent strength that is never far below the surface. There are curses of despair in the scene of her capture, but the final note struck is one of composure and even faint hope:

> I am arm'd 'gainst misery:
> Bent to all swaies of the Oppressors will.
> *There's no deepe Valley, but neere some great Hill.*
>
> (III, v, 167–169)

The concluding line is not without significance. The noble and dignified behavior, the majesty in adversity, which the admiring Bosola attributes to the Duchess at the opening of Act IV, is the reaction of a woman who is inuring herself to pain and misery, but who has so far refused to sink into despondency. Her hope, played upon so expertly by Ferdinand and clung to so eagerly by her, is not irrevocably shattered until she sees the counterfeit bodies and takes the dead man's hand to be her husband's. It is then that she breaks down in despair, it is then that she curses her brothers and even the stars.

There can be no doubt about this interpretation of the scene. By depriving the Duchess first of her elevated social position, then of her liberty and the amenities of life and now finally of her hope, Webster has methodically taken away all the exterior supports on which she may conceivably have relied to fortify her endurance. From now on she is all alone in a closed room, with nothing outside herself to aid her. What follows should logically be the ultimate trial. "The Robin red-brest, and the Nightingale, Never live long in cages" (IV, ii, 15–16).

The Duchess' ordeal is not the simple horror sequence for

which it is still occasionally mistaken and on which aspect we have so far concentrated. Her reactions are subtly and significantly varied. She leaves the stage cursing, with her composure gone and her spirit apparently broken, whereupon the gloating Ferdinand takes over with his "Excellent; as I would wish" and "she'll needes be mad," as if to stress the natural consequences of the treatment she is going through. But when the Duchess is next seen, she is in perfect command of herself, using the very devices of her tormentors to steel herself against their attacks. Again, and not for the last time, Webster resorted to a technique of ironic reversals, partly no doubt in order to create tension within the act.

But there was more than questions of technique and tension to be considered. The central problem involved in the presentation of the Duchess was as always psychological and thematic. She should show weakness, otherwise she would become dangerously dehumanized and unlikely to be regarded as "one of us" by any conceivable audience. She should also display strength, otherwise the implications of her stand against the law and might of her brothers would become irreparably blurred. From this important point of view a pattern of action with both ups and downs had also much to recommend itself. But it had to develop in a definite direction: the Duchess should be humiliated only to be raised up higher.

The final prison scene demonstrates, perhaps somewhat surprisingly, that Webster was keenly aware of the psychological aspect of the problem. The abruptness with which the "weakness" shown by the Duchess at the sight of the wax figures is changed into the composure with which she faces the madmen, does not preclude hints about how this composure is acquired. In her conversation with Cariola before the madmen enter there is a notable new element of introspection:

O that it were possible we might
But hold some two dayes conference with the dead . . .

(IV, ii, 22–23)

It is through this introspection that she should be understood to have reached complete realization of her plight and accepted it as something inevitable, something that must be borne:

> Necessity makes me suffer constantly,
> And custome makes it easie—
>
> (IV, ii, 31–32)

The self-dramatization that normally accompanies such intense contemplation of one's own situation is not forgotten by Webster. "Who do I looke like now?" (IV, ii, 32) "And Fortune seemes onely to have her eie-sight, To behold my Tragedy" (37–38) and "For I am chain'd to endure all your tyranny" (64) are striking expressions of this state of mind. Nor are the exigencies of human nature lost sight of in the reactions of the Duchess to Bosola's bewildering conduct. She clings to a dignity that is now an illusion only—"I am Duchesse of *Malfy* still" (IV, ii, 139); there are touches of fear and wonder in her attitude to the gambols of her executioner—"Let me be a little merry" (148), "Why, do we grow phantasticall in our death-bed?" (151); there is simple pathos in her expression of concern for the children and stark horror in the exclamation that momentarily breaks through her armor of self-control—"any way, (for heaven sake) So I were out of your whispering" (228–229). There is the natural turning to religion and the assumption of a kneeling position in preparation for the execution, followed by the final wish for the sleep of death. In the shadow of death Webster's heroine becomes indeed a credible human being.

The thematic importance of this psychological credibility has already been pointed out: by such means the dramatist made the Duchess remain a character with whom the imaginative spectator could identify himself without doing violence to probability. A representative aspect of her tragedy was thus kept alive and in full effect.

But Webster goes beyond this, and he does it in a highly

ingenious manner. The same insistence of the Duchess on her princely dignity that was just now called human and natural, also serves to remind the audience of the greatness she inhabited when the play opened. Her self-dramatization serves a double purpose: by making her so naturally direct all attention to herself Webster builds up the significance of her trial and power to endure it, he makes her as it were stand out in relief—Duchess of Malfi still. The ultimate isolation from story and milieu, essential to the condition of most tragic heroes, is then achieved by what is really an extended self-dramatization—by the use of "expansive" soliloquies where pregnancy of thought and suggestiveness of language transcend the situation and take us far beyond the scandals of the Aragonian family and the petty plots of Matteo Bandello. The prison where "Th' heaven ore my head, seemes made of molten brasse, The earth of flaming sulphure" (IV, ii, 27–28), where prisoners have their throats cut with diamonds, are smothered with cassia and shot to death with pearls, is not located at Amalfi but anywhere and everywhere.[4] In this prison the Duchess submits to her fate with dignity and humility:

> Pull, and pull strongly, for your able strength,
> Must pull downe heaven upon me:
> Yet stay, heaven gates are not so highly arch'd
> As Princes pallaces—they that enter there
> Must go upon their knees: Come violent death,
> Serve for *Mandragora,* to make me sleepe.
>
> (IV, ii, 237–242)

In her last speeches Webster makes his heroine proceed by associations that come very close to being conceits, and it is largely through these abrupt and compelling associations of poetry that he achieves his most vital effect: to force the audience to consider the general significance of what they are watching. From the psychological point of view the Duchess may be acting a part, but it is the central part in the masque-like show that Bosola is directing, and it is most fitting that the show should end in as emblematic a fashion as possible.

The elevation of the Duchess above the level of ordinary human beings at this her last appearance is incontestable. But what is the significance of the elevation, what is the emblem of which she is the central part? The arrangement of the bodies when the murders have been performed indicates the correct interpretation: the somewhat ambiguous Cariola is carried into the next room, while the bodies of the children are displayed together with their dead mother. The crucial question "Alas, how have these offended?" (IV, ii, 273) is asked and rapidly settled by the comments first of Ferdinand—why did not Bosola oppose himself "Betweene her Innocence, and my Revenge" (297), and then of Bosola:

> Oh sacred Innocence, that sweetely sleepes
> On Turtles feathers.
>
> (IV, ii, 383–384)

No matter how praise and blame had been distributed earlier in the play, in the final prison scene, at the moment of her death and for ever afterwards, the Duchess is regarded as innocent. Through the device of poetic elevation she even becomes a representative of innocence, and her death, as contemplated by herself and the audience and because the dramatist wills it so, a martyrdom. We are finally allowed to see the Duchess as Antonio saw her in the first scene of the play:

> Her dayes are practis'd in such noble vertue,
> That sure her nights (nay more her very Sleepes)
> Are more in Heaven, then other Ladies Shrifts.
>
> (I, i, 205–207)

In this shifting of emphasis onto the innocence of the Duchess, the strident notes in which she once defended her natural right to marry Antonio must necessarily be absent. Only once and quite early in the act is the issue explicitly referred to and hardly in a simple and straightforward manner:

> FERD.   where are your Cubbs?
> DUCH. Whom! FERD. Call them your children;
>   For though our nationall law distinguish Bastards

From true legitimate issue: compassionate nature
Makes them all equall.
DUCH. Doe you visit me for this?
You violate a Sacrament o'th' Church
Shall make you howle in hell for't.

(IV, i, 40–47)

The Duchess' reliance on the sacrament of marriage at this point is in marked contrast to her self-sufficiency in the wedding scene, with its challenging references to the church. It is now Ferdinand who ironically states the case for the defense on which she formerly relied, a curiously inverted theme that may or may not recall the original statement of the law of nature, "the stay of the whole world," as Webster calls it in a later play.[5] But the power of the imagery does not allow us to forget the issue. "The Robin red-brest, and the Nightingale, Never live long in cages" is the continuation and sad conclusion of the most daring expression of the "nature theme" in *The Duchess of Malfi:*

The Birds, that live i'th field
On the wilde benefit of Nature, live
Happier then we; for they may choose their Mates,
And carroll their sweet pleasures to the Spring.

(III, v, 25–28)[6]

This is the issue kept alive. When the Duchess lies dead with her children, violence has been done not only to innocence but also to nature.

"Now that I wake." Critics have maintained that *The Duchess of Malfi* should really have ended with the death of the heroine, that its plot has the serious defect "of reaching its natural end before the play."[7] There are good reasons for this complaint, but it should also be remembered that, in spite of the title, Webster chose to make it Bosola's tragedy as well. The death of the Duchess is the decisive event in his life; it is around her fate that his argument with Ferdinand turns; her conduct has in fact

conditioned his attitude as much as have his employer's commands, and it continues to do so after her death. Thematically no break occurs, and the act runs on until Bosola announces his intention to leave for Milan—a decision that provides a much-needed physical link with the events that follow.

It is clear that Bosola's attitude to the Duchess, ambivalent already at the time of her capture, has definitely changed at the time of Ferdinand's first efforts to bring her to despair. Not only does he now discern "the shape of lovelinesse More perfect, in her teares, then in her smiles" (IV, i, 8–9), but having observed her closely during the early stages of her ordeal, he is now full of admiration for her. To what extent this admiration should be understood to modify his conduct is, however, a moot point. In the first scene of the act his advice to her, though obviously disingenuous in substance, seems straightforward enough. "Come, you must live" (IV, i, 81), "Leave this vaine sorrow; Things being at the worst, begin to mend" (91–92), "Come be of comfort, I will save your life" (101)—these exhortations are, superficially considered, best explained as efforts to keep the Duchess' spirit of resistance alive. But when we begin to inquire into the motives behind these efforts, the problem becomes more obscure. Bosola's pity for his victim may be genuine, but why is he trying to make her look toward the life she hates rather than towards the death she desires? He may be hoping against hope that Ferdinand will finally set her free—" 'Faith, end here: And go no farther in your cruelty" (IV, i, 141–142); he may also sincerely want her to maintain her poise and dignity, to maintain, as it were, his own idea of majesty in adversity. But Bosola builds hope and dignity only to break it down: when the Duchess changes her tune from desperate grief to desperate curses, his taunts provoke her, force her to consider for one tense moment the abysmal hopelessness of her situation—"Looke you, the Starres shine still"—and then spur her on until she leaves the stage both cursing and longing for death:

Let heaven, a little while, cease crowning Martirs
To punish them:
Goe, howle them this: and say I long to bleed—
"It is some mercy, when men kill with speed.

(IV, i, 130–133)

If we should understand as Bosola's intention the strengthening
of the Duchess' determination to endure, his efforts must be
deemed an absolute failure and the comment with which Ferdinand enters must have a particularly hollow ring in his ears.

But this "Excellent; as I would wish: she's plagu'd in Art"
points to a much simpler explanation, which is undoubtedly the
correct one. Knowing well that Ferdinand is watching the proceedings, Bosola carries out his instructions to the letter; throughout his interview with the Duchess he is plaguing her in art.
This excludes neither admiration nor pity for her, but such
considerations do not interfere with his management of the situation. He is still the loyal servant of his master; when his rashly
given promise never to see the Duchess again runs counter to the
interests of Ferdinand, he equivocates it away, exchanging it for
a new one that is equally open to a double interpretation:

when you send me next,
The businesse shalbe comfort.
FERD. Very likely!

(IV, i, 163–165)

Such quibbles are more remarkable at this stage of Bosola's
career than appears at first sight. He has really no right to quibble.
With the capture of the Duchess his original debt of loyalty to
Ferdinand has been amply paid—his intelligencing days are over
and the provisorship of the Duchess' horse is no more—but he
remains in his master's employment and in a capacity that he
knows may well involve the murder of the Duchess. Webster
skips the striking of this new bargain, but he makes its terms
perfectly clear: Bosola will receive his pay upon the satisfactory
completion of his terrible mission. The master-servant relation-

ship is thus drastically shorn of its inessentials and ambiguities and reduced to a practical agreement between two self-interested parties. Nevertheless it is depicted as a living reality to Bosola. He may, in the final analysis, murder the Duchess and her children for money and advancement only, but now as before he prefers to look upon himself as acting under a bond of loyalty to Ferdinand.

It is in conformity with this bond that Bosola faithfully and painstakingly executes the measures conceived by his employer for the final ordeal of the Duchess. His comments voice his characteristic, almost professional disgust with the general state of mankind, but they are also designed to bring the victim by degrees to mortification; from his announcement "I am come to make thy tombe" to the bellman's song they stress the vanity of life and the immediacy of death:

Thou art a box of worme-seede, at best, but a salvatory of greene mummey: what's this flesh? a little cruded milke, phantasticall puffe-paste: our bodies are weaker then those paper prisons boyes use to keepe flies in: more contemptible: since ours is to preserve earth-wormes: didst thou ever see a Larke in a cage? such is the soule in the body: this world is like her little turfe of grasse, and the Heaven ore our heades, like her looking glasse, onely gives us a miserable knowledge of the small compasse of our prison.

(IV, ii, 123–131)

It is in answer to the Duchess' questions that Bosola descants on his theory of life, in perfect accordance with which he is now tormenting a woman whom he deeply admires. But when she even now refuses to break down, it is he who asks the question which, in pursuit of the argument that started within him long ago, has repeatedly come to the surface in his reflections and to which the Duchess' conduct could possibly yield the answer: is there after all a justifiable alternative to a completely self-centered way of life? As he realizes that there is, he seems to develop a desire to keep his victim's dignity intact even at the moment of her death. No such respect is shown Cariola and the children. Whatever pity Bosola is supposed to feel during the executions, he expresses none until they are over.

This unsentimental interpretation of Bosola is the only one undoubtedly supported by the text and also the only one that satisfactorily explains his reactions when Ferdinand spurns him as a common murderer. For his rejection by the Duke is at least as important as the moral conversion that Bosola is gradually undergoing. He has fulfilled his part of the bargain; by rejecting him Ferdinand refuses to honor his part, he is "falling into ingratitude" and subjecting Bosola to the same treatment as his brother the Cardinal had done before. The two are accordingly rightly coupled together in their agent's denunciatory speech:

> Your brother, and your selfe, are worthy men;
> You have a paire of hearts, are hollow Graves,
> Rotten, and rotting others: and your vengeance,
> (Like two chain'd bullets) still goes arme in arme—
> You may be Brothers: for treason, like the plague,
> Doth take much in a blood: I stand like one
> That long hath ta'ne a sweet, and golden dreame.
> I am angry with my selfe, now that I wake.
>
> (IV, ii, 344-351)

Although these remarks have a general reference to the state of moral corruption in which the Aragonian brothers live, they also refer specifically to Bosola's personal grievance. Like the Cardinal before him, Ferdinand has now violated the principle of loyalty according to which, superficially at least, Bosola has arranged his life. The "sweet, and golden dreame" that he has taken is the assurance that this principle will not be broken, that he will be paid for being rather "a true servant, then an honest man" (359). This loyalty is, I take it, the "painted honour" that he now casts off in order to turn to the moral principles with which his conscience has been continuously plaguing him. The Duchess' conduct *and* Ferdinand's ingratitude settle the argument within his mind.

This explanation is in harmony with the reactions and reflections that make up the soliloquies with which Bosola closes the act. Even with the dead Duchess before his eyes he is not allowed to argue his case out in unequivocal terms of good and evil. Extraneous elements enter repeatedly. He is made to excuse himself as an unwilling instrument of necessity—"that we cannot be suffer'd To doe good when we have a mind to it" (IV, ii, 387–388), to refer piteously to the pangs of conscience, the "sencible Hell" that he feels, and even to tremble before the actual hell that he sees yawning. His attempt to revive the Duchess, the embodiment of innocence that he hopes will prepare the way "to take me up to mercy," and his decision to enact something "worth my dejection" are thus described as brought about by a combination of circumstances. This makes the process of the conversion psychologically convincing. It may also leave alive some dramatically beneficent doubt about how much Bosola's dejection will be worth when strong action in the defense of virtue is required.

Final Conflict and Final Statement

An Ending Accomplished. According to Belleforest's story only one episode remained for Webster to stage after the murder of the Duchess: Bosola had to stab Antonio to death—an incident that could hardly be extended through a whole act. An Elizabethan dramatic story was, however, subject to rules that did not govern an Italian novella, at least not to the same extent. Where Bandello could treat his series of events as a sequence within the continuous flow of history and, together with his readers, assume that the Aragonian brothers went on to unspecified fresh fields of operation, Webster could leave no such obvious loose ends. The audience had to be informed of what happened to every major character in the story and preferably not in the makeshift form of an epilogue but in full stage representation. The story had to be finished and finished in style. The murder of Antonio was only one incident. Equally important matters had to be taken care of.

Dramatic practice, whether caused by conviction or convention, also guided the kind of conclusion to which a dramatist could

resort. According to Belleforest, if not Bandello, the characters
that survive Antonio are all villains—the Cardinal, his brother,
Bosola—and villains were not allowed to remain unpunished,
hardly even alive, at the end of an Elizabethan tragedy. Some sort
of moral justice had to be meted out, and of the alternatives available Webster clearly chose the natural one when he had this
murderous trio killed off.

But although major evildoers had to be requited according to
their deserts, the choice of method to achieve this was free.
Within the comparatively narrow framework that the story of
Vittoria Accoramboni offered, Webster certainly managed to prepare his villains for execution with both subtlety and art. In *The
Duchess of Malfi* he enjoyed greater liberty, being able to direct
the activities of the characters step by step in each individual case.
Ferdinand, the Cardinal, Bosola, and partly Antonio, could be
manipulated according to the themes of the play rather than in
conformance to a fairly rigid historical plot. The argument going
on within Bosola's soul need not lack dramatic illustrations.

The redirection of interest, essential to the structure of the play
after the climactic prison scenes, is achieved in the brief conversational episode with which the last act opens. By clarifying both
Antonio's situation and the measures that he contemplates, Webster establishes two facts that will determine the subsequent development of events: the Aragonian brothers do not "mean well
to Antonio's life," but nevertheless the poor man intends to
"venture all his fortune" on a nightly visit to the Cardinal. To
the audience that has just witnessed the murder of the Duchess,
his hopes cannot but seem delusive:

> It may be that the sudden apprehension
> Of danger (for I'll goe in mine owne shape)
> When he shall see it fraight with love, and dutie,
> May draw the poyson out of him, and worke
> A friendly reconcilement.
>
> (V, i, 75–79)

The ineffectiveness, the insufficient knowledge of the ways of the world, which is so characteristic of Antonio, has here been carried to excessive lengths. His innocence, like Marcello's in *The White Devil,* verges on culpable naïveté. There is, however, also a note of desperation present in the speech ("better fall once, then be ever falling") which indicates that this time Antonio's deliberations will lead to action and a direct clash with his enemies; the echo scene that follows only confirms this impression. The victim of the persecution of the Aragonians is thus made to maneuver himself into a position loaded with dramatic possibilities. The conflict must come to a head, but the exact direction in which it will develop cannot be foretold.

One of the threats to Antonio's life seems, however, to have disappeared. The distraction that afflicted Ferdinand at the sight of the bodies of his sister and her children is now elaborated into full-fledged stage madness, described as lycanthropic by the doctor in agreement with hints earlier in the play, but in no way specified as such in the actual ravings of the patient. It is of course eminently fitting from the retributory point of view that the violent and spasmodic Ferdinand should be studying the art of patience, but otherwise the theme of madness seems rather indifferently handled, with elements of incidental fun and satire perfunctorily introduced. Such an apparent defect may, however, serve a sensible purpose. This is a mad scene where pathos must be avoided, and the introduction of ludicrously irrelevant conversation is a safe way of doing this, while at the same time the essential aspect of the episode is underlined: "what a fatall judgement Hath falne upon this *Ferdinand*" (V, ii, 83–84). The obligation of the dramatist to show retribution at work has thus been fulfilled and an attractive "universal truth" plausibly maintained.

But Ferdinand's affliction also serves a far from ignoble structural purpose. By demonstrating the utter irrationality of the Duke's conduct Webster introduces an unpredictable element into the final conflict. He is actually putting himself in a conveniently commanding position: he can now handle the violent Ferdinand almost gratuitously, bring him on and make him behave according to no rules but those of his own making. Another clash is thus prepared for. Ferdinand may be mad, but he is not out of action.

As a guardian of the Aragonian family interests, however, he is no longer to be reckoned with. The responsibility for punitive measures against Antonio has come to rest solely on the Cardinal. His competence seems unquestionable, since "He's nothing else, but murder," and the first steps that he takes look highly practical, but the audience knows that he labors under the fatal misconception that Bosola's services can still be secured for gold or a promise of advancement. When he also underestimates the importance of his mistress' emotionalism and overestimates his own ability to outwit her, the Cardinal is left with more on his hands than he bargained for. Instead of having only Antonio to kill, he has now Julia's body to dispose of and both Antonio and Bosola to kill, a change for the worse which seems, mockingly, to indicate a certain fallibility even in a Machiavellian's plans. Nevertheless he proceeds to lay new ones, and with the dangerous Bosola as his agent.

Bosola's attitude to the Aragonian brothers must be regarded as settled by Ferdinand's rejection of him, even though some doubt persists about how much his "dejection" will eventually be worth. His ambiguous reply to the Cardinal's command—"I would see that wretched thing, *Antonio* Above all sightes i'th' world" (V, ii, 148–149)—obviously indicates that his determination to reform holds, an impression confirmed by his readiness to use Julia as a tool against his new employer. He never seriously contemplates re-entering the Aragonian service: his desire to find a master of a worthy caliber is as feigned as his promise to kill Antonio, whereas his objections to a further pursuit of "fortune" and "seeming Honor," which are dismissed as "mellancholly" by the Cardinal, are genuine. The vacillation that can still be detected

in his words is caused by such secondary considerations as are
activated by his desire to mend his ways. There is the question
of personal safety:

> O poore *Antonio*, though nothing be so needfull
> To thy estate, as pitty, Yet I finde
> Nothing so dangerous: I must looke to my footing;
> In such slippery yce-pavements, men had neede
> To be frost-nayld well: they may breake their neckes else.
>
> (V, ii, 365-369)

These scruples are overcome by the same combination of arguments that secured his conversion: a sense of justice, sincere
remorse and hope for redemption. But a new possible course of
action is soon introduced: Bosola may join Antonio in a "most
just revenge." This alternative, a natural extension of the plans
of a reformed cutthroat, is not rejected, and it adds another
element of uncertainty to the clash of wills and interests towards
which the intrigue is made to move. When the Cardinal assures
himself of privacy in order to carry out his designs, the stage is
set for this final encounter. Bosola, his supposed tool, has plans
of his own. Ferdinand and Antonio, the madman and the innocent, are no respecters of privacy.

Of these four major characters none survive the catastrophe
and, in accordance with the Bandello and Belleforest story,
Antonio is the first to go. But his fall has a peculiar Websterian
logic about it, far removed from any source and any average
dramatic solution: the apprehensive Bosola, mistaking him for
the Cardinal and excited by Ferdinand's lurking in the dark, runs
him through most expertly—Antonio, "The man I would have
sav'de 'bove mine owne life" (V, iv, 62). By this "direfull mis-
prision," for which he conveniently blames his desire to "Imitate
things glorious," he has played into the hands of the Cardinal.
As far as Bosola personally is concerned, the situation is, however, easily reversible. A professional cutthroat, armed with a
deadly weapon, is now to confront an adept schemer, unarmed

and cut off from help. The Cardinal will indeed be brought to the hammer.

At first everything seems to develop to Bosola's satisfaction. The Cardinal, a victim of the trap he has himself prepared, is being mercilessly slaughtered by his own hired murderer. But then the unpredictable appears again in the figure of Ferdinand, and this time with truly decisive consequences. The madman slays both schemer and agent, thus throwing into utter confusion all their plans for aggrandizement, personal safety, or atonement. For the dying Bosola it only remains to make his revenge perfect by dispatching Ferdinand, the "maine cause" of his undoing. Thus the villains and their tool are allowed to die in the proper order, with proper dying speeches on their lips, whereupon, with some justification, Delio can introduce Antonio's surviving son as a ray of hope in the darkness and end the play on the most affirmative note available:

> *"Integrity of life, is fames best friend,*
> *Which noblely (beyond Death) shall crowne the end.*
>
> (V, v, 145–146)

Futility or Hope? The somewhat conventional theme of retribution, with which the last act of *The Duchess of Malfi* is mainly concerned, certainly did not prevent Webster from bringing his play to a technically satisfactory conclusion. He clarifies the situation after the heroine's death, redefines the conflicting forces and brings the two major ones together in a tentative measure of strength, which is resolved in a sequence of ironic twists of chance. After this "rehearsal" he arranges the more complex final clash in the same fashion, with well-laid schemes repeatedly and ironically frustrated. The desirable slackening of pace after the catastrophe is painstakingly observed and the important concluding note prepared for. The act as a whole, built out of almost nothing, is a good testimony to Webster's professional skill.

This is faint and perhaps somewhat premature praise to lavish on the last act of one of the great Elizabethan tragedies, and to commend Webster for the thoroughness with which he brings his villains and their associates to a bad end, is to add little more. Complexity of plot and simplicity of theme is a common Elizabethan combination, particularly in revenge tragedy. The main question is: how is the theme developed through the plot, or, to be more specific, how does the methodically applied pattern of scheme versus counterscheme, with its reiterated reversals of fortune, affect the moral impact of the act?

The irony of these reversals is persistent and striking. The procedure is the same in the episode between the Cardinal, Julia, and Bosola as in the ultimate encounter between the four main adversaries: to raise the expectations of the schemer by presenting him with an illusory golden opportunity, only to dash them conclusively at the moment of apparent success. Studied from this point of view the act becomes a sequence of plans that miscarry, not because they are foiled by more ingenious ones, but because something unexpected always intervenes. A complete confusion of success and failure, aims and consequences seems to reign. Chance decides, and, in a resigned spirit not unlike Montaigne's, intellect counts for nothing.[8]

It is important to realize that the pattern is not a moral one. Good and evil characters alike suffer from this frustration of plans. Antonio's failure as peacemaker is just as decisive as the Cardinal's as manager of bloody events, and the problematic Bosola succeeds, not as supporter of the virtuous, but rather as self-satisfied revenger. The theme of retribution that occupies Webster throughout the act is simple only if superficially considered. No religious significance can be extracted from it, for the perversity of superhuman intervention is demonstrated as thoroughly as is the bankruptcy of human intelligence. The Aragonian brothers are killed, but so is Antonio. Not only does providence lack a tool in *The Duchess of Malfi,* it does not operate, even in the form of nemesis. What governs the events is

nothing but chance, independent of good and evil, physics and
metaphysics, and symbolized most appropriately in the figure
of a madman. Webster's use of ironic reversals is thus part of a
larger scheme: plot and theme combine and cooperate to produce
a final effect of unrelieved futility, foreshadowed several times in
the past by Bosola's bitter denunciations of the world.

The game of chance emerges so clearly, with Ferdinand playing
a central part in it, that only little verbal elucidation is needed in
the tragedy. It is obvious to Bosola that Antonio dies from "Such
a mistake, as I have often seene In a play," and his previous
reflections indicate that Webster wanted him to be at least partly
conscious of the pattern that is developing:

> We are meerely the Starres tennys-balls (strooke, and banded
> Which way please them)—
>
> (V, iv, 63–64)

But as the pattern demands that neither Bosola nor the Cardinal
should desist from scheming and promoting their schemes, their
consciousness of the muddle that chance is making of their lives
must be limited. Bosola's "fate" must press him on in spite of his
knowledge of the ways of the world, and the Cardinal's guilty
conscience must not overwhelm him. They cannot be allowed to
realize the futility of their efforts, until these efforts have been
brought to an absolute close and they themselves lie dying.

No such considerations need interfere with the thoughts to
which Antonio gives voice. As he ascribes no value to his "poore
lingring life," his expressions of resignation and despair can be
given a more general significance; they can be made to carry the
mood of the play, as Bosola's merciless unmasking of the pretensions of mankind has done earlier. Antonio has indulged in such
expressions before—"Heaven fashion'd us of nothing: and we
strive, To bring our selves to nothing" (III, v, 97–98)—but in the
echo scene the aspect of futility is elaborated in so determined a
manner that the resignation at which Antonio has arrived cannot

but color the remainder of the play. In the verdict on life that he
delivers as he lies dying, it has become more than a mood; it is
stated as a theme, an interpretation to be accepted or refuted:

> In all our Quest of Greatnes . . .
> (Like wanton Boyes, whose pastime is their care)
> We follow after bubbles, blowne in th' ayre.
> Pleasure of life, what is't? onely the good houres
> Of an Ague: meerely a preparative to rest,
> To endure vexation.
>
> (V, iv, 75–80)

In spite of his reflections on hell and the tediousness of a guilty
conscience, the Cardinal is not made to join Antonio in this
sweeping condemnation of the pursuits of man, and he dies without having advanced further than a realization of his own individual failure, even though his final wish to be laid by and never
thought on naturally sounds the familiar note of absolute futility.
Not so Bosola. As befits a man who has always adhered to a
cynical interpretation of human motives and who has already
come to suspect that we are the stars' tennis balls, he paints an
even more somber picture of the world than did the dying
Antonio:

> We are onely like dead wals, or vaulted graves,
> That ruin'd, yeildes no eccho: Fare you well—
> It may be paine: but no harme to me to die,
> In so good a quarrell: O this gloomy world,
> In what a shadow, or deepe pit of darknesse,
> Doth (womanish, and fearefull) mankind live!
> Let worthy mindes nere stagger in distrust
> To suffer death, or shame, for what is just—
> Mine is another voyage.
>
> (V, v, 121–129)

"A shadow, or deepe pit of darknesse"—this is indeed an appro-
priate description of the world in which the Aragonian brothers,
Antonio, and Bosola have been groping in the last act of *The
Duchess of Malfi*. The characters themselves may realize their

predicament late, or not at all, but the audience is made well aware of the probability that all the efforts, brave or treacherous, will only end in death and disaster. Action and speech combine to make this plain. In a final analysis of *The Duchess of Malfi* the theme of futility, as developed in the last act, is obviously of central significance.

The theme is not a novelty in Webster. Even in the bustling, energetic world of *The White Devil* people die with words of resignation and despair on their lips—Vittoria contemplating her soul "driven I know not whither" and Flamineo groping "in a mist," actually reaching a conclusion that is closely paralleled in Antonio's last sad speech:

"This busie trade of life appeares most vaine,
"Since rest breeds rest, where all seeke paine by paine.[9]

But the characters in *The White Devil* are defiant, even if it is with the flamboyant courage of the desperate. They may occasionally falter in their self-sufficiency, but they always express it convincingly—Lodovico glorying in the successful limning of his night piece and Flamineo stating the ideal bluntly, as a challenge in the teeth of death:

I doe not looke
Who went before, nor who shall follow mee;
Noe, at my self I will begin and end.[10]

It is obvious that the Duchess' determination to remain "Duchesse of *Malfy* still" is a significant variation on this stoical theme. For once in Webster it becomes possible to identify the self-realization of a character with the integrity of life which, in Delio's words, *"noblely (beyond Death) shall crowne the end."* Of the plea for the integrity of the ego, an attitude perhaps largely inspired by Montaigne, very little remains in *The Duchess of Malfi:* Julia is the only character to die in something resembling the grand old manner.[11] The plea is in fact notably twisted; first by the dying Antonio when he realizes that his life and death are perfectly matched, and then by Bosola when he puts the career of the Cardinal to the ultimate test:

> I do glory
> That thou, which stood'st like a huge Piramid
> Begun upon a large, and ample base,
> Shalt end in a little point, a kind of nothing.
>
> (V, v, 95–98)

To this the self-realization of *The White Devil* has finally come. Without integrity of life it is reduced to an absurdity, a kind of nothing. Bosola may glory in his deeds, in his "Revenge, for the Duchesse of *Malfy,* murdered by th' Aragonian brothers" (V, v, 102–103), as if this revenge was a design that he deliberately set out to accomplish. But the play tells otherwise. It is through a combination of good intentions, opportunity, and cutthroat habits that Bosola manages to take his revenge in "so good a quarrell." He dies as he has lived, murderous and neglected. His self-realization is thus more complete than Webster has made him aware of.

Bosola's reversal to his old self—he also dispatches Antonio's servant most professionally—adds significantly to the impact of the murders in the last act of *The Duchess of Malfi,* particularly if they are compared to the death of the heroine. They are not elaborately staged, the victims are not projected in heroic isolation, the ritual of execution is completely absent. What we witness is instead how an expert murderer corners his defenseless quarry, how the latter cries out for help, tries to escape, begs for mercy and is repeatedly stabbed by his pursuer. Then there follows a general scuffle, with large wounds inflicted by a raving maniac, and finally Bosola's convincing application of the finishing stroke to Ferdinand. This is the violent death that comes to the villains of *The Duchess of Malfi.*

It could hardly have been described in uglier colors. A cut-throat, a coward, and a madman—to these the final struggle reduces Bosola and the Aragonian brothers. Deliberately, almost mercilessly, Webster denies them the end granted Vittoria and Flamineo, not to mention Zanche and Julia. In perfect harmony with the gloomy picture of the condition of man that Bosola paints in his last speech, not even the redeeming feature of bravado is left this world to brag of.

Bosola is, however, not only concerned with the actual state of the world but also with its possible remedy. In his penitence for the death of the Duchess he has tried to apply exclusively ethical standards and act accordingly; that he has failed repeatedly through the interference of others and the habits that have become second nature to him does not change this basic fact. He sees himself striking with the sword of justice and dies with a ringing assertion of established moral values:

> Let worthy mindes nere stagger in distrust
> To suffer death, or shame, for what is just—
>
> (V, v, 127–128)

It is of course primarily the example of the Duchess but possibly also that of Antonio that comes to the spectator's mind, when he hears Delio sum up his interpretation of *The Duchess of Malfi* in the familiar extolment of integrity of life with which the play ends. The careers of the Aragonian brothers are equally relevant, as foils and negative examples. But Bosola is at the core of the argument: not only does he conduct it in thoughts and words, he lives it. As he undoubtedly interprets it, it is his career that, with the Duchess' example before him, speaks most persuasively in favor of true integrity of life.

This hopeful interpretation is strongly supported by what actually happens as the play closes. Antonio's surviving son is brought in by Delio, who enjoins everybody to establish him in his mother's rights. An indication of confidence in the future? Perhaps. No Francisco de Medicis is lurking ironically in the shadows this time. The villains are all dead, leaving "no more fame behind 'em, then should one Fall in a frost, and leave his print in snow" (V, v, 139–140). As the "pritty gentleman" is the son of Antonio and the Duchess, his virtue should be secure and he must be expected to grow up to become a "Lord of truth." With far less ambiguity than in *The White Devil* moral integrity is accepted as the true guiding principle of man's life; its representatives even seem to be on the way toward establishing a duchy of virtuous living where evil triumphed before.

Of the desirability of this project there can be no doubt, but Delio's words involve no more than a promise that sincere efforts to realize it will be made. As was the case in *The White Devil*, prevailing facts speak eloquently against the expectation of a tolerably virtuous future on any but the most limited scale. Here as in Shakespeare's great tragedies the effect of the ending primarily depends on what has preceded it. The death of the Duchess may be said to represent a triumph of virtue as well as *virtù*, but only *sub specie aeternitatis*, a truly chilling perspective. The miserable failure and death of the Aragonian brothers may similarly be said to cancel out the undoubted success of their schemes to eradicate the offenders of their family honor. But no such facile balancing of good against evil can delete the impact of Bosola's career on the audience. For his own interpretation of it does not contain the whole truth. In spite of his conversion, even in the execution of "a most just revenge," he remains the creature of his former deeds—actually demonstrating the full extent of Webster's exploration of the theme of futility while arguing the case for complete integrity of life. The two themes are not reconciled in *The Duchess of Malfi;* they are deliberately juxtaposed. Integrity of life is fame's best friend, but mankind also lives, womanish and fearful, in the deep pit of darkness from where no conceivable integrity will help us up.[12]

VII ❀ A Jacobean Tragedy

Theme and Psychology: Webster's Characterization

In the preceding elucidation of the meaning of *The Duchess of Malfi* each major dramatic figure has received particular attention at one stage or another and, although characterization has not been the aspect of Webster's art under discussion, some idea should have been gained of his methods to achieve it. Abstraction was clearly seen at work, and it was on the whole acknowledged to be successful. The play makes sense; elementary rules of psychological verisimilitude are observed and, with the exception of Bosola, the characters seem unusually simple and clear-cut. How was this combination of import, simplicity, and plausibility obtained?

The figures in *The Duchess of Malfi* that are most obviously presented as epitomes of abstract ideas, as character types rather than individuals, are the Aragonian brothers. As long as the Cardinal is kept in the background, appearing only for brief but revealing exchanges with Ferdinand, he remains an impressive representative of arbitrary evil in power. But as he is forced to fight for his reputation and life against the prying Bosola, it becomes impossible to keep him aloof from the petty incidents of the intrigue. Now the master Machiavellian begins to shrink, and he is soon reduced to a small-minded improviser of crimes, with a limited vision and a limited field of operations. The grand command he is supposed to sway over the imperial army at Milan is conveniently forgotten; he gives no orders and has no staff officers to put his plans into effect. Instead of having Bosola hewn to pieces, he meets him on a most disadvantageous ground, is trapped like any "old Fox" and finally killed. A sad ending for a dignitary who "should have beene Pope" and who "strewes in his way Flatterers, Panders, Intelligencers, Athiests, and a thousand such politicall Monsters" (I, i, 161–163).

In the process of "cutting the Cardinal down to size" Webster concentrates on a side of his character that has not been developed before: now he is really "growne wondrous mellancholly," far beyond the expectations raised by Antonio's early description of him. He would like to pray, but the devil takes away his heart; he is puzzled in a question about hell and plagued to tediousness by a guilty conscience, being finally convinced that

> I suffer now, for what hath former bin:
> "Sorrow is held the eldest child of sin.
>
> (V, v, 73–74)

It is a logical and thematically satisfactory solution to have this brooding villain sink deeper and deeper into his misery until he only wishes to be "layd by, and never thought of," his spirit broken by the forces within him. It is also a psychologically convincing development. But Webster does no more than sketch it: Bosola's is the only mind worth detailed attention at this advanced stage of the play. Thus the Cardinal, although dethroned from his seat of power and drastically "humanized," disappears in death, leaving behind him a definite impression both of the destructive power of evil within society and the self-destructive power of evil within the human mind—the latter aspect being, as far as I can see, the main reason why Webster made his churchman melancholy and not only secretive, as he is in Belleforest. The "humanization" had to take place to make some tentative boring into his soul possible, but a proper distance also had to be maintained so as not to upset the balance of interest. This is carefully observed by Webster, who uses his most suggestive poetry to apply the necessary touches, with the fortunate result that the Cardinal does not lose all symbolic stature, nor does he slip into the oblivion that he longs for. Instead he haunts us, continuously puzzled in a question about hell and continuously threatened by a thing armed with a rake that seems to strike at him.

Ferdinand constituted a different problem. From the first the two brothers are contrasted but, whereas the Cardinal is made to remain in Rome, Webster focuses attention on Ferdinand by making him confront his erring sister at Amalfi. But no elaboration of his character takes place. The Duke's fits of passion only confirm and exemplify Antonio's original analysis of him as "a most perverse, and turbulent Nature" and make him appear the epitome of uncontrolled violence that is obviously required by the argument of the play. As a psychological portrait Webster's Ferdinand is primitive, simplified to the point of caricature, in spite of the felicity with which his cast of mind is occasionally described:

A very *Salamander* lives in's eye,
To mocke the eager violence of fire.

(III, iii, 59–60)

It has been generally observed that Webster prepares for the outbreak of lycanthropy by making Ferdinand's mind run on the subject of wolves before he actually goes mad; but not that he also indicates how this mental breakdown is a natural crumbling of the unbalanced mind that the Duke, with his limited intellectual powers and preoccupation with sex and violence, has always been described as possessing. Ferdinand is a potential maniac: finally these two themes gain the upper hand to the exclusion of all other thoughts and he loses control of himself— a consistent and, in general terms, psychologically credible development.

The steps by which Webster makes his violent prince descend

into the darkness of his soul are noteworthy. He enters the Duchess' "last presence Chamber" gloating over his revenge and seems to remain unmoved by the spectacle of the dead children, but when he fixes his eye "constantly" on his sister, the youth of her face strikes him and then the horrible thought that "should I die this instant, I had liv'd Her Time to a Mynute" (IV, ii, 284–285)—a firmly self-centered basis for the collapse that follows. Not until Ferdinand has finally put himself in the place of his victim does he realize the significance of his deed, and then can remorse begin to do its work. A frantic search for defensible motives takes place; he turns in despair on Bosola but, even while the latter is contemptuously rebutting his arguments, his mind begins to wander and he leaves distracted, to "hunt the Badger, by Owle-light" (IV, ii, 360).

This is both shrewdly observed and, within the narrow space that can be devoted to the disintegration of a stage villain's mind, convincingly executed. In the subsequent mad scene there are some painful excrescencies, which, however, do not exclude the application of effective touches to the Duke's character. Here, as in the two brief appearances he still has to make, suggestive comments are mixed with pure nonsense in the best Elizabethan tradition, so that an impression is created of a mind that is not only shattered by the atrocious past but still somehow in contact with it, haunted by it and tortured by it.[1] Ferdinand's "My sister, oh! my sister, there's the cause on't" (V, v, 90) can thus be accepted as psychologically possible, which is hardly the case with his final couplet:

"Whether we fall by ambition, blood, or lust,
"Like Diamonds, we are cut with our owne dust.
(V, v, 91–92)

At this stage of the play psychological considerations matter little. The characters behave according to parts assigned them by the author in his capacity of conductor of the concluding argument of *The Duchess of Malfi*. The combined effect is all, the individual inconsistency nothing. It is, however, notable that although no character is treated more dangerously in the abstract than Ferdinand, Webster manages at the critical moment to "humanize" him in the same manner as he does his brother. By slowing down the pace of the action when the decisive deed in Ferdinand's career has been committed, he is able to concentrate on his mental reactions and thus make a thematically required development psychologically credible.

Antonio is naturally more frequently on the stage than either Ferdinand or the Cardinal, but—in contrast to what is the case in Belleforest—he is never allowed to dominate it. In social status he is no match for the Aragonian brothers, in strength of character no match for the Duchess, and in intellect no match for Bosola; after having served as introducer of others he is accordingly made to play second fiddle in his encounters with them. He has his moments of dignity and his moments of embarrassment, but they are moments only. Between his glowing description of the Duchess to Delio and his departure from wife and children outside Ancona, attention is never focused on him for long, and his motives and reactions are hardly analyzed at all. Consequently we tend to forget his attractive qualities and remember his deficiencies, as we sense rather than see a development from hesitancy and inefficiency to melancholy and resignation, clearly within the scope of the character but with too few pertinent details filled in to make the process intriguing. Not until the last act is Antonio allowed to hold the stage and then almost entirely as a *Stimmungsfigur*. As such he is essential to the total effect of the play, but the psychological entity that is Antonio no longer matters. Not even here do we come close to him as a human being, and consequently his character, although viewed as a unity virtually from beginning to end, remains a portrait executed in preponderantly general terms of a weak but well-meaning gentleman.

This is disappointing in at least one important respect. As a technical protagonist of the play Antonio should certainly receive greater attention, explain himself or be explained by others to a greater extent than now; otherwise the audience will lose interest in him, no matter how often he is on the stage—as we actually come close to doing. Webster was, however, faced with a difficult problem, similar in nature to that which confronted him in the case of the Cardinal but considerably more complicated. The thematically significant concept of Antonio is that of an indubitably virtuous man of average personal ability, who is overwhelmed by events with which he is not equipped to cope. This combination, this balance between weakness and good intentions, had to be maintained, or one of two distressing consequences might ensue: either the Duchess' choice or Antonio's conduct would appear inexplicable. Webster's way out of this dilemma was, I take it, to keep a certain distance to the major-domo, enter only superficially into his mind and leave the delicate problems of his intimate motives and responses largely unsolved. As far as I can see, any other solution would have interfered dangerously with the argument of the play, threatened to overshadow the figure of the Duchess or called for a more detailed study of character than any known type of Elizabethan drama admitted.

This is to explain and not to justify. The uneasiness which the spectator feels before Antonio will abide with him, even after he has reconciled himself to the unheroic qualities of this "hero." It remains incongruous to have considerable if intermittent interest devoted to the psychological processes of the Aragonian brothers but none at all to those of Antonio. A few more subtle and provocative touches could easily have been applied to him. Antonio fits into the argument of *The Duchess of Malfi*—he is even essential to it—but from the point of view of characterization he is perfunctorily handled. Theme, I would say, too obviously overshadows psychology, and psychology suffers: not fatally, not even unreasonably, but in part at least unnecessarily.

The character of the Duchess is from the very first differently treated. She is made to hold her own in the difficult verbal skirmish with her brothers and then launch out into a ringing challenge of them, directed not to Cariola but to the audience:

> Shall this move me? if all my royall kindred
> Lay in my way unto this marriage:
> I'll'd make them my low foote-steps.

> (I, i, 382–384)

There is no subtlety about this, no analysis of her emotional state. Webster is interested primarily in the thematic impact, not in psychological verisimilitude. But in this way she is established as a center of attention, a figure of sufficient stature to attract and hold the eye, and a bold sketch of her is given that can be gradually filled in with enough details to make her come alive as an independent stage character.

This is what Webster proceeds to accomplish in the wooing scene. There is still no analysis, no concentration on any one aspect of her character; instead the details are added impressionistically in the course of a conversation that develops with surprising plausibility from the casual and playful to the significant and serious. Several things are done at once and psychological completeness is not attempted; thus the portrait of the Duchess remains a sketch, but more precise, charming, and suggestive than before.

The same economical impressionistic technique is used in the bedchamber conversation between the Duchess, Antonio, and Cariola that follows in Act III. The heroine is again shown in high spirits, although the background is now one of happiness and contentment and the span of her observations accordingly limited. But this is a fleeting expression of an ephemeral mood; with the entrance of Ferdinand everything is utterly changed; joy and charm vanish and sorrow and strength enter in their stead. The process is not studied: one side of her character is, as it were, turned away and another faces us, both of them easily contained within the personality that Webster has made us envisage, but no integration is attempted. There is no time for it and perhaps no real necessity either. The "elliptical" technique, largely based on the effect of some of Webster's most expressive poetry, is obviously successful, for when the Duchess is captured by Bosola she is already "arm'd 'gainst misery," and we accept the transition unquestioningly.

From now on, however, ellipsis has no place in the presentation of the Duchess. In the prison scenes everything that happens to her is staged before our eyes and nothing left to the imagination. There are excellent thematic reasons for virtually everything that the Duchess says and does in these scenes, and some violence to psychological probability might accordingly be expected. But her conduct is both significant and credible. She is not all determination and dignity: Webster has given her touches of curiosity, fear, and womanliness, so that the princess who suffers "constantly" in Act IV becomes recognizably the same person as the high-spirited widow who woos Antonio in Act I and the wife and mother whose happiness is threatened by Ferdinand in Act III. Considering the brief moments in which he defines and individualizes her personality, Webster's Duchess is one of the great achievements of Elizabethan kaleidoscopic characterization. The portrait is suggestive rather than factual, mystifying rather than logical, as a natural consequence of this technique. Yet where unity and verisimilitude are maintained, as they are in the case of the Duchess, this is altogether an advantage.

Bosola is the only character in *The Duchess of Malfi* whose psychological processes seem at all consistently exhibited—not unexpectedly, as the outcome of the play hinges on the mental conflict that somehow leads to his conversion to a better cause. It is easy, however, to overdramatize the struggle between the two souls within his breast. There is no mystery about him; it is wrong to turn him into a sort of common man's Hamlet, except as a center of attraction for all sorts of ideas associated with his plight. As long as the Duchess is alive, Bosola goes through the motions of a struggle rather than fight it out, for the outcome is every time determined in advance by compelling motives of personal advantage. The possibility of a change of mind must be established and thus Webster makes him talk about his qualms quite freely, but, no matter how emotionally described, they are never presented as influencing his choice. For all his vaunted search for an ethical principle in life, Bosola remains a determined but expertly rationalizing egoist until his conversion takes place. This is the light in which Webster makes us view the character, and that is what gives it the psychological unity it undoubtedly possesses.

The "conversion scene" is the one in which Bosola's mental processes are revealed with the greatest minuteness. The picture given of his mind is far from simple: ethical considerations alone are not made to sway him, nor is the emotional impact of the Duchess' death described as the decisive element. These factors contribute to the conversion, but he does not desert the Aragonian cause until Ferdinand "falls into ingratitude" by refusing to honor his part of their bargain. Taken on the rationalizing level, where Bosola explains his motives and deeds to himself and the audience, this makes excellent sense. Taken on the more complex level of actual human behavior, where egoistic and altruistic motives mingle and a hard-to-define emotional response to the whole situation decides the issue, it is equally convincing. On both levels Webster's Bosola impresses us as a closely observed and deeply disturbing character study.

The technique used to achieve this effect is a combination of Webster's approaches to other key characters in *The Duchess of Malfi*. Attention is centered on one episode, one psychological process, which is followed in as intimate detail as is dramatically feasible—notice that the parallel reactions within Ferdinand's mind receive comparatively short shrift. No logical step-by-step analysis of motive and choice is attempted, even though Bosola has the privilege of the audience's ear to an extent shared by

no one else. Instead revealing information is given in a seemingly arbitrary fashion, as meandering thoughts and meandering
conversation bring up new subjects—a method of clarification
used with great success in the case of the Duchess. It is obviously
not without its dangers: on one hand casualness may be carried
so far that only confusion follows, on the other provocative compression of thought and expression may lead to distressing
artificiality. This does not happen in *The Duchess of Malfi*: not
even when the repudiated Bosola attempts to evaluate his new
position in life, is verisimilitude thrown to the winds. His reactions to the belated last gasps of the Duchess determine the
tenor of his soliloquy, within which the thoughts follow each
other rapidly, in a disjointed fashion that perfectly reflects the
pressure under which his mind is understood to be working.
The language fits the thoughts: brief, incisive, emotionally
charged sentences, not without jarring notes of sentimentality
and self-pity. Everything falls into place, and Webster's portrait
of Bosola, the habitual rationalizer of motives, becomes more
lifelike than ever.

The consistency with which the five significant characters of
The Duchess of Malfi are presented is, as we have now seen,
remarkable. With the exception of Antonio each figure is designed to make a strong impact on the audience at an early
stage; few, important and unmistakable qualities are stressed so
that the association with significant abstract concepts becomes
clear, and then the figure is maintained within these well-defined
outlines until the end. The main reason for this procedure is
undoubtedly thematic, but the result is that a striking unity of
character is achieved also from the psychological point of view.

This is not altogether to the advantage of the play. Every time
the Aragonian brothers appear, the same characteristic traits are
elaborated with increasing precision, until their conduct becomes
almost comically predictable, particularly that of Ferdinand.
Psychological unity is achieved, but largely, I would say, through

psychological simplification. The method of radically abstract characterization that is used so blatantly in *The Revenger's Tragedy* is for once approached in *The Duchess of Malfi*.

The chief reason why Webster manages to avoid turning all his figures into Tourneuresque puppets is neither that he willingly compromises with the demands of his theme, nor that his sense of psychological verisimilitude asserts itself irresistibly. What more than anything else contributes to the impression of recognizable human beings that his characters convey is his habit of suddenly concentrating attention on a particular process within a particular character's mind and his genius of finding the right words for it. Antonio is the only one who—for far from contemptible reasons—is not accorded this treatment, but the method is used to restore some human proportions to Ferdinand and to give the audience at least the illusion of an understanding of the Cardinal's soul.

But the success of Webster's excursions into psychology grows impressive only when the effects obtained in the cases of the Duchess and Bosola are considered. In his treatment of the heroine's last minutes Webster evinces a profound and acute insight into her predicament so poignantly that her conduct becomes both significant and credible in the midst of the extraordinary horrors he assembles. His ability to persuade the audience to accept the fact of Bosola's conversion after having had him toy with the idea for so long provides similar evidence, not only of his psychological acumen but also of his skill in using it when he found it in the interest of his tragedy to do so.

For psychology is of course never an end in itself in *The Duchess of Malfi,* no matter how capable of keen observation and subtle commentary Webster is. It is subordinate to the play's argument, even though it may at times support it so eloquently as to make the processes in a character's mind come alive and the character somehow assume the proportions of an independent study. Here lies the great virtue of Webster's kaleidoscopic characterization. The impact of the crucial episodes—the Cardinal deep in thought, Ferdinand repenting, the Duchess plagued in art, Bosola arguing out his case—remains with us, and by force of this we, the audience, are led to believe that we are witnessing a conflict between considerably more complex persons than actually appear on the stage. This illusion is essential. Suggestive abstraction, the application of touches of psychological insight and sudden poetic expressiveness—these are the means by which Webster creates his characters. On the whole they play their parts convincingly, pieces in a game of chess and pathetically human figures at the same time.

Theme and Action: Webster's Sensationalism

The conclusion that the forms which the main figures of *The Duchess of Malfi* assumed were determined more by thematic considerations than by Webster's concepts of psychology is hardly unexpected. What is surprising is rather the general plausibility and occasional subtlety of the characterization, which goes far to show that, when it came to necessary artistic compromises, Webster knew how to strike a proportionate balance between conflicting demands. His art seems casual (some critics prefer harsher terms) but it may be a casualness which, for all its defects, does the play no irreparable damage.

Let us for instance consider his use of the common dramatic conventions of aside and soliloquy. On the whole they have been cut to the necessary minimum: the major characters are equipped with confidants—servants, friends or partners in crime—and have thus no need to communicate their thoughts directly to the audience.[2] The only exception is Bosola, about whose inner struggle the others must be kept in the dark so as not to endanger the structure of the latter half of the play. Consequently Webster makes him take the audience into his confidence, thus establishing the rapport between speaker and listener without which the significance of his conflict might have failed to be understood.

Whether deceiver or deceived, whether villain or victim, he remains under the audience's close observation, and this largely through Webster's judicious use of the conventions of aside and soliloquy, to whose more sophisticated possibilities he had paid but little heed in *The White Devil*.

A similar concentration on essentials is noticeable in other aspects of Bosola's character, particularly if he is compared to Flamineo, who is generally accepted as his counterpart in *The White Devil*. They both give voice to incidental satire, but in *The Duchess of Malfi* this is confined to two or three episodes, and the stream of words which flowed so freely in the earlier play has largely been checked. There is no such "monkey-business" as set quarrel scenes and formal embracings in *The Duchess of Malfi*: although the conventional aspect of Bosola is unmistakable, he does not follow the pattern so closely as do Malevole and Vendice and also to a great extent Flamineo.[3] Because of his intimate bond with the audience there is no distinct dividing line between his "garbe of mellencholly" and the uncompromisingly moral attitude which he occasionally strikes: they are at the same time expressions of his character and part of a dramatically plausible device to hold up an inner conflict for reiterated consideration—an ingenious use of an easily abused convention.

Webster's achievement in the sphere of over-all planning and plot management is perhaps not so readily appreciated, the scenes being occasionally strung together in a seemingly haphazard fashion. Little perspicacity, however, is needed to discover that Act I has been molded into a generally satisfactory shape. After Antonio's introductory analysis of the conditions at the French court the action moves smoothly and unobtrusively, without awkward breaks and overelaboration of details, cleverly preparing the ground for the secret wedding ceremony, of which the probable consequences are also made clear. With the possible exception of Antonio's flippant introductions, nothing extraneous acts as an impediment to a proper following of the argument of the act.[4]

It is true that, once Belleforest's Aragonian brothers were made to transfer their activities to Amalfi at this early stage of affairs, the material at hand lent itself well to the writing of an act of striking unity. But the subtle continuity that marks it cannot be accounted for in this manner, nor has its nature always been properly recognized. Webster's sense of timing and motion seems to be the decisive factor. Until Antonio and the Duchess are brought face to face, the characters are kept constantly moving, in an apparently casual manner, and while Delio and Antonio are watching this procession go by, they are now drawn into conversation with others, now left alone to deliver their apposite comments. In this way threatening gaps are bridged and the procession can go on without becoming tedious or even obvious. The convention of the independent introducer had been mastered, not merely followed.

And the processional method is not used for introductory purposes alone. The leading characters withdraw, only to reappear in new combinations: Bosola with the Cardinal, Ferdinand with courtiers, Ferdinand with Bosola, the Duchess with her brothers, with Ferdinand, and alone, with Cariola, and with Antonio. A constant grouping and regrouping of characters is taking place, until their relationship is made clear and the latent conflict envisaged. It is all managed with skill and plausibility, and the thematically important contrasts strike home effectively. And then follows the wooing scene, opened innocently enough as yet another of the conversation pieces of which this conversational act is made up, but rapidly developing into the crucial incident of the whole play. After motion and small talk, stillness and ceremony; after threats and misgivings, decisive action. Matter and form are joined together in a manner beyond the reach of mere professional competence and sophisticated habits of thought. Granted that the problems involved in the construction of Act I of *The Duchess of Malfi* may not have been of the major order, the subtlety and thoughtfulness with which they have been solved are nevertheless impressive. Action and argument seem perfectly united.

The problems of the two subsequent acts are quite different. In the middle of Act II the scene shifts from Amalfi to Rome, and at both places the exigencies of the plot make it necessary to deviate from the simple time sequence followed in Act I. The Duchess must have time to give birth, Delio to reach Rome and the Aragonian brothers to be told of their sister's predicament. This means separate, relatively brief scenes, divided by intervals marked by an empty stage—in short, the episodic treatment of action that is so characteristic of the Elizabethan drama. The technique obviously puts as heavy demands on the dramatist's competence as any other. Since Act II of *The Duchess of Malfi,* with its compression of time and sudden change of scene, can be presented as a homogeneous, swiftly moving sequence without creating obscurity or confusion, Webster must have solved the basic technical problems adequately.

This is not to make unprecedented claims for the dramatist's skill, nor would such be appropriate here. The act is not a master-piece, not even a notable success. For all its thematic justification, Bosola's baiting of Castruchio and the Old Lady is an awkward method to stretch unrewarding material as far as it will go. A similar lack of balance characterizes the subsequent scenes, in which the irrelevant and the ludicrous demand our attention to an uncomfortable extent. To create dramatic suspense around the secret birth of a child is clearly a thankless task, but the alarms and excursions resorted to by Webster, which culminate in the dropping of the horoscope, are inordinately clumsy, no matter what the significance of the horoscope itself.[5] This is casualness carried too far—as if the dramatist were saying that this or at least something of the sort must have happened and left it at that. The Amalfi scenes should dominate Act II, as it is still at the Duchess' court that the important events occur, but owing to Webster's perfunctory treatment of them the interest actually tightens when we move from the action at Amalfi to the reaction in Rome.

No comparable excrescencies mar the sequence of Act III, where the happy family life of Antonio and the Duchess, the irrevocable discovery of their secret, their escape from Amalfi, expulsion from Ancona, and final separation provide enough material for even a very sketchy dramatic treatment. Structurally the act follows the pattern of its predecessor, with sudden changes of scene and a time scheme that is still more tightly compressed. But a mere variation of Bosola's intelligencing activities is avoided, and the threads of the intrigue get more tangled than before, as is proper when what little plot there is in *The Duchess of Malfi* moves towards a climax. The decisive complication is achieved through Ferdinand's "right dangerous" visit to his sister's court, with the situation brought to a head in the tense bedchamber interview. This is a brief episode, but it is prepared for and elaborated as the real moment of crisis it is. Henceforth a struggle to escape is all that remains to the lovers.

Webster manages the scene with great dexterity. Not only is Ferdinand's interruption of the idyllic family conversation presented with shocklike intensity, but Antonio's indecision, his wife's unpremeditated decision for him and her lack of defense against Bosola's wily attack follow each other with natural ease. So plausibly is it done that the audience scarcely realizes that Ferdinand's failure and Bosola's stroke of luck are separated by a few minutes only, during which interval the Duke conveniently sees fit to depart post-haste for Rome. Again Webster allows coincidence a wide berth, but this time with considerable success—a verdict that also applies to the act as a whole. Belleforest's story is naturally simplified, but this is so sensibly done that the dialogue can proceed with about the same degree of elaboration throughout—except in the curious scene at the shrine of Loreto. This is handled in a manner that immediately sets it off from the rest of the act, if not from the rest of the play. From the point of view of plot it is hardly necessary, with its conversation between two pilgrims, its ditty and its dumb show, but it illustrates graphically the essential contrasts between the forces that oppose each other. Here, as in the subsequent parting scene, Webster resorts to emblematic presentation, demonstrating, as it were, the virtues of the flexible Elizabethan dramatic practice in the hands of an intelligent writer. As used in *The Duchess of Malfi* the convention of the dumb show makes it possible to reach a thematically important effect in a most economical way. Compressed symbolic action, rather painfully lacking in *The White Devil*, is employed here with conspicuous success.

In Act IV Webster reverts to a simple time scheme and, using only one necessary break between scenes, devotes the whole act to the murder of the Duchess, its preliminaries and immediate consequences. Such a concentration on one event naturally brings with it detailed presentation and elaborate staging; here, where the prison walls restrict the movements of the characters, it also means a slow pace of action, an impression of *stasis* rather than *dynamis*. Time stands still, as it should do when the heroine dies. In this important respect Webster's handling of the situation is admirable and should not be difficult to appreciate.

And the whole act is well managed, with unobtrusive technical competence, many provocative touches of great subtlety and a thoughtfulness that should no longer surprise. It is not only an extended torture and execution scene that we witness; Webster is deliberately taking the Duchess, Bosola, and Ferdinand through the consecutive stages of an extended debate on the vital issues of the play. Short spans of tension and minor ironic reversals bring the action forward until it has been demonstrated that the spirit of the Duchess cannot be broken, to which demonstration her murder is the natural climax. Then the debate shifts ground; confronted with their own handiwork Ferdinand and above all Bosola are put to a test from which they emerge decisively changed and with their old spirit broken. The interest in Bosola, developed gradually by Webster from its feeble beginnings at the opening of the play, is now sufficient to let him claim the center of attention, as befits a character that must carry the argument embodied in the Duchess to the conclusion envisaged by the dramatist. Thus the transition to the final act is managed, perhaps not smoothly enough from a perfectionist point of view, but, considering the difficulty of the problem, in an eminently satisfactory manner. With all its lurid ingredients this deceptively simple-looking act is one of the most complex products of Elizabethan dramatic art. It may also be one of its minor triumphs.

The contrast between the obvious logic and unity of Act IV and the mercureal shifts of its successor is immediately apparent. The shifts do not mark any significant compression of time; they are made largely to bring the chief characters along separate converging lines into fatal collision with each other. Not only is this problem solved, but complications are introduced that keep the spectator sufficiently in doubt about what is going to happen next to maintain his interest in the plot. For once in *The Duchess of Malfi* a cloak-and-dagger game is being played, and certainly in no inept fashion. And yet the meaning of it all is not obscured, it is inherent in the intricacies of the plot. Again action and argument are convincingly joined, and this time the process was not a simple one.

So far, so good. Although *The Duchess of Malfi* has its awkward moments and is not comparable to *The White Devil* in tension, thrills, and spectacular incidents, the action is on the whole presented competently and judiciously, with some regard for immediate stage effect but more for the demands of the argument. But our discussion has been limited as if the play contained nothing but generally approved dramatic fare, and mention has only occasionally been made of the strong ingredients of sex and violence which have caused critics to describe it as impermissibly shocking and its author as a deliberate speculator in pornography.[6] The phenomenon cannot be explained satisfactorily by references to changing standards of conduct, common Jacobean stage practice, or any other combination of historical circumstances. Webster and his contemporaries may have taken a "healthy Renaissance interest in sex," but this did not force Webster and Shakespeare to introduce Julia or Lucio as figures in serious drama. They lived in a violent age and the theater made much of violence, but this did not compel them virtually to exterminate the dramatis personae of such plays as *Hamlet* and *The Duchess of Malfi*—for Webster's tragedy is, let us hope, closer to *Hamlet* than to *Titus Andronicus*. The approach to the dramatist's sensationalism must now be critical rather than historical, and his efforts accepted, rejected, or simply tolerated on their merits within the play. This means applying one's own ethical and esthetic standards to notoriously delicate matters, but there is, as I see it, no other path leading out of this familiar Websterian wilderness.

The violence in *The Duchess of Malfi* occurs in formidable, highly concentrated doses. With their slow pace and detailed presentation the prison scenes constitute a concentration of intensely unpleasant effects that has few parallels in serious dramatic literature, and in Act V the carnage, with its spice of madness added, is at least as extensive as in the last act of *King Lear,* a play whose story admittedly carries more weight. It is understandable that critics have deemed it necessary to characterize the elaboration of the climax and concluding events in *The Duchess of Malfi* as bedlam-broke-loose and their creator as either irresponsible or "possessed by death."

As we have seen how deliberately Webster puts his violent effects to thematic use, such a sweeping condemnation is unwarranted: the prison is not a Neapolitan chamber of horrors, and the Milanese murders add up to much more than "una caotica carneficina." [7] The elements against which objections are legitimately raised—wax figures and madmen, bell, coffin and cord, poisoned bibles, armed lunatics and locked-in victims—may be too crude, too melodramatic or too elaborate, but they serve Webster as tools only, although of an unusually convincing nature. Everything outrageous that happens in the last two acts of *The Duchess of Malfi* may in fact be defended on thematic grounds. Webster's use of violence is unmistakably subservient to the argument of the play.

The aspect is important and the defense valid, but only within carefully observed limits. Although the nature of the Elizabethan drama made constant maintenance of realistic verisimilitude unnecessary, plausibility in the form of a judicious balance between dramatic means and dramatic ends had to be observed. Even a highly accomplished writer ran an obvious risk whenever he exploited violence at great length or with great intensity. Undesirable reactions to the horrors he presented might frustrate his bravest tragic attempts.

Seen in this perspective Acts IV and V of *The Duchess of Malfi* assume a different complexion. Ferdinand's madness, Julia's intrigue with Bosola, and the Cardinal's self-imposed helplessness all serve recognizable serious purposes, and yet the episodes produce questionable effects. Again we have a case of Elizabethan "casualness" to contend with: the workmanship seems at times so slipshod and the stage trickery so crude that wholehearted immersion in the play's argument is needed to accept what is happening as possible even in the hectic world of *The Duchess of Malfi*. For no compelling reason the dramatist threw verisimilitude to the winds and fell back on comfortably conventional behavior patterns for Ferdinand, Julia, and the Cardinal, with results that might easily have been as embarrassing as the dropping of the horoscope in Act II. The misfortune is probably averted by the rapid pace and great economy with which each incident is presented; the dramatic emphasis falls elsewhere, and what in itself verges on the ridiculous becomes acceptable within the unusual frame of the act. That the impression of "una caotica carneficina" lies near at hand is, however, undeniable. The finale of *The Duchess of Malfi* is a tour de force that will always require delicate handling on the stage.

The danger that threatens in Act IV is somewhat different, but the reactions of the audience are equally hard to predict. To watch the torturing of the heroine without shudders of horror is probably impossible, but as all manner of strange things are done to her, the shudders may well turn to embarrassed laughter —the seriousness and ingenuity of it all may become a little ludicrous.[8] Passive suffering is in itself dangerous as a tragic theme; to attempt effects of exceptional intensity in a situation based on the defenselessness of the victim craves unusually wary walking.

Webster cannot have been unconscious of these dangers. In the early Jacobean drama there is a marked striving for advanced horror effects, with results that are at times so ambiguous that one wonders whether Mr. Eliot's interpretation of *The Jew of Malta* as a farce might not with equal justification apply to works by Barnes and Chettle, Marston and Tourneur. In *The White Devil* Webster had himself tried his hand at stage horrors and been in a position to observe their impact on the audience. Now he must have known what he wanted and, in spite of the risks involved, set out to achieve it. Thus we get an extension of Brachiano's death scene in the torture and murder of the Duchess, and a complication as well as an extension of the struggle between Vittoria, Flamineo, and Lodovico in the final settling of accounts between Antonio, Bosola, and the Aragonian brothers.

A conspicuous predilection for intensified effects, then, characterizes Webster's dramatic art in *The Duchess of Malfi,* a conclusion that should suffice to justify the common classification of him as a decadent writer. Comparatively few critics, however, restrict the application of the term to such technical matters. It is instead frequently used to imply a moral evaluation of the dramatist: he must be morbid, otherwise he would not persist with such gruesome spectacles. This verdict was particularly easy to reach, as he also showed an improper interest in the unpleasant aspects of sex.

Outspoken love scenes and references to sexual matters may of course serve thematic needs to exactly the same extent as death scenes and references to heaven and hell. Two episodes in *The Duchess of Malfi* stand out as being largely concerned with the controversial subject, and of these Bosola's discourses to Castruchio, the Old Lady, and Antonio are extended to such lengths and in such a direction that they become commentaries on life rather than on love. Julia's part, on the other hand, is almost exclusively concerned with sexual behavior: she is, if we wish to make the point, guided by the two forces of lust and avarice. Thematically, however, she is of little importance until the last act. Then her role assumes critical proportions, as her abrupt courting of Bosola caricatures the Duchess' conduct in the wooing scene in word and deed. The parallel was, as I see it, intended by Webster as an ironic example of where "nature" may lead if not accompanied by virtue. In spite of the strikingly similar way in which they behave, an essential distinction is made between Julia and the Duchess, between the little woman of pleasure and the great woman in love. The episode seems to serve a highly laudable purpose.

But the effect is, regrettably enough, most uncertain. Only a vague parallel to the Duchess' deportment is offered; its significance is never spelled out. Instead of the condonation of the secret marriage that I see there, harsh criticism of her as an irresponsible voluptuary may be implied: everything depends on how the rest of the play is interpreted and on our idea of how flexible an attitude to the pertinent moral problems Webster's contemporaries entertained. The parallel is too ambiguous to be accepted as conclusive.[9]

And excessive ambiguity is not the only defect from which the episode suffers. Whatever its moral point may be worth, it is

made at a badly chosen moment. Long before Julia begins to ogle
Bosola, reader and spectator alike have formed definite opinions
about the Duchess' conduct, and neither praise nor blame, be it
open or implied, will now affect their judgment. Julia's escapade
comes too late and can only cause bewilderment. Although her
death serves its limited thematic purpose better, it is also largely
redundant. Futility would reign, even though her blood were not
shed.

This may well be the main deficiency of the last act of *The
Duchess of Malfi.* For all the painful effect of Ferdinand's capers
with the doctor, it was in connection with the development and
termination of the intrigue between the Cardinal, Julia, and
Bosola that Webster's Jacobean ideas of dramatic art led him in
the most perilous direction. By overstating his case where modera-
tion was called for and blurring thematic outlines where precision
was needed, he tended to create the impression that he had either
lost control of his subject or was actually pandering to the desire
of the audience for sensational and pornographic effects. Webster's execution of the details of the by-plot is obviously far from
ideal. More remarkable, however, is the fact that his concept of
what an important dramatic ingredient would achieve was criti-
cally at fault. This makes the artistic balance of the act somewhat
questionable. The general tenor of the argument is almost too
easy to appreciate, while the thoughtfulness and subtlety that is
also in it may pass virtually unheeded. Only if the audience is
willing to listen carefully to the modulations of the dialogue, will
the full meaning be perceived of the follies and atrocities that,
superficially considered, constitute the act. This is a demand that
the Elizabethan drama often makes upon us. It is unusually
difficult to conform to it here, but also unusually rewarding. The
complex and problematic last act of *The Duchess of Malfi* is a
worthy companion to its more easily appreciated predecessor.

It is possible that my explanation of Julia's part has been too
tolerant. The dramatist may actually have gone far out of his way

in order to create a series of episodes of a thoroughly popular quality and paid only casual attention to the thematic confusion that would inevitably follow. But the possibility matters little. Julia does not appear in carefully prepared key scenes but in vividly sketched ones, and, as we noted, undesirable by-products have little time to develop dangerously. The crucial episodes, where any gratuitous exploitation of violence and sex would be most keenly felt, are those in which delicate or ambiguous situations are elaborated with all the peculiar intensity at Webster's command: Bosola's onslaught on Castruchio, the Old Lady and Antonio in Act II, and the Duchess' torture and death in Act IV.

In spite of the great merits of the prison scenes and the meticulous care with which they were planned and executed, some doubt remains about their ultimate effect. The combination of macabre paraphernalia, passionate interest in the conduct of the victim and her complete defenselessness undoubtedly contains an element of calculated appeal to the morbid instincts of any audience, which accounts for the nervous reactions that the scenes easily call forth. The experiment in dramatic presentation that Webster is conducting takes place in the border region between the tragic, the pathetic, and the ludicrous, and the effect that he achieves has consequently a strong element of the grotesque. This is one of the qualities that is most firmly associated with Webster's art, and quite rightly so. Whether it adds significantly to the tragic sense of *The Duchess of Malfi* is, however, another matter. If the dramatist had followed a safer course and used less *outré* ingredients, he would, as far as I can see, have accomplished essentially the same results. This is a blasphemous conclusion to arrive at in a discussion of a major Jacobean drama, but one from which I see no escape. Webster's obsession with death is real, but is not therefore at the heart of his dramatic thought.

The other crucial episode, Bosola's performance as professional malcontent in Act II, is outside the action of *The Duchess of Malfi;* it interferes with the tempo of the play in much the same way as does an even more typical *Stimmungsszene,* Antonio's and Delio's conversation with the ominous echo. In the latter, however, the mood is developed economically and poetically, whereas Bosola is made to hold forth at length and in the jerky periods of Websterian prose, only once breaking out into poetic "meditation." Although the discourses help to characterize the speaker and are often neatly turned and picturesquely phrased, their main task is to establish the background of mood without which the Duchess' character and conduct cannot acquire their full significance. Our picture of the Aragonian world largely depends on the sentiments and attitudes that its servant and representative voices.

In this respect Bosola's harangues serve their purpose. A remarkable intensity is maintained while repulsive physical aspects of human existence are gleefully analyzed, and at the climax an almost excremental view of life is expressed, as lice and worms, "the most ulcerous Woolfe, and swinish Meazeall" are used to bring home to the audience the close relationship between man's true nature and that of the wild beasts. The great are like the humble—"there's the same hand to them"—all equally contemptible. On this basis the validity of decent human motives is naturally denied and man reduced to the bestial level. To quote the proverb paraphrased by Webster in *The White Devil:* man to man is a wolf.

There can be no doubt about the prurience of several of Bosola's tirades; he is deliberately made to explore human filth, to some extent at least for the delectation of the spectators with a taste for such fare. This is done with an inventiveness that does credit to Webster's insight into certain tendencies of the human mind, but also with an insistence and repetitiveness that becomes boring. Bosola's discourses stand out from the rest of the play in a disturbing fashion: they tend to become independent essays on human behavior. Although they develop the atmosphere of vice and corruption which surrounds the Duchess and thus contribute to the inner unity of the play, there is a coloratura aspect to them that simultaneously threatens its artistic balance.[10]

The remedy would seem to have lain close at hand. By judiciously cutting Bosola's malcontent sallies and meditations and by resorting to poetic condensation of the essential observations they contain, Webster could, I believe, have accomplished the same effects in a more economic and less exasperating way. More suggestiveness and less documentation—this is how Bosola is used elsewhere in *The Duchess of Malfi,* and nothing in any sense beneficial to the play seems lost. Bosola fails as a stage character when he is most conventional; if Webster had been more independent of contemporary dramatic practice, he would certainly have further modified the volubility of his master commentator— another step away from the quite irrepressible Flamineo in *The White Devil.* Still, the voluble Bosola is with us; even when we condemn his speeches as supererogatory, we take them for granted as expressing something essential to his character and the play. Here, as in the prison scenes, it is perhaps weakness too much to think what should have been done.

On this ambiguous but largely affirmative note the examination of Webster's use of sex and violence may appropriately end. The questionable elements are there for everybody to see: some effects are perfunctorily developed, others are carefully contrived but in an uncomfortably eccentric direction, the Julia by-plot is mainly an excrescency. Opinions will always differ on how disturbing these defects are. Some adjustment to them is probably necessary for every spectator. One does not have to accept the grotesquerie of Webster's art in order to appreciate *The Duchess of Malfi,* whose essence may be largely independent of this aspect, but a realization of its existence smooths the way towards an understanding of the tragedy. Everything falls into place more easily. The horrors of Acts IV and V, some of which will always seem childish, become more closely related to a central argument that is consistently mature. Ferdinand's dirty jokes and Bosola's vicious sallies become largely responsible for creating a mood of great tragic significance. The brutal world of the Aragonians is the nightmarish background against which the Duchess' conduct and character are made to stand out. Even though we refuse to be carried away by Webster's most blatant efforts, we must admit that the grotesque does him yeoman service.

The creation of the atmosphere of evil is intimately connected with what might be called the representational value of the action of *The Duchess of Malfi,* an aspect where the play has been said to fail conspicuously.[11] If the mood is not persuasive, we are witnessing nothing but a stage presentation of an insigificant anecdote about the unwise second marriage of an obscure Italian princess, from which an unusual but far from unique moral in the tradition of the medieval *exemplum* is drawn, and to which the many arresting observations that are made have only an accidental relationship. If the mood succeeds, the play acquires a meaning beyond its sordid story: it becomes a dramatic illustration of the prevalence of lust and violence, arbitrary force and wanton cruelty. Such is the normal state of the world. Man to man is a wolf. There can be no doubt that this effect is abundantly achieved in *The Duchess of Malfi.* The illusion keeps us spellbound. Here the defense—for a defense it has become—of Webster's sensationalism may finally rest.

Tragic Sense and Tragic Impact: The White Devil *and* The Duchess of Malfi

To have reached such a favorable conclusion on the most controversial elements of which *The Duchess of Malfi* is composed may seem strange after the criticism that we have also leveled at the play. A few explanatory words are thus called for. In every instance, I believe, the criticism points to conditions that will continue to disturb readers and prove embarrassing on the stage, if they are not handled with circumspection. This state of affairs, however, does not indicate a dismal artistic failure by the author or reflect the sad plight of the medium in which he wrote. In an Elizabethan tragedy many things were usually attempted at the same time, with the result that compromises between the various desiderata became necessary and shortcomings in one respect or the other almost inevitable. It was in the nature of the drama to condense and sketch, to expand and elaborate, even to exaggerate and distort, all in the interest of what the author considered important in the individual scene or for the total effect. The balance that could be achieved in such a way was certainly not classical, but Shakespeare's example goes far to show that it provides a workable basis for the writing of great tragedy. The potentialities of the Elizabethan drama are extraordinary. It is also kind to authors who have something worthwhile to offer.

And Webster's significant contributions are, as I have indicated, by no means limited to explorations of those aspects of life in which the satisfaction of lust, avarice, and ambition plays the principal part. In *The White Devil,* a tragedy where every major character follows his desires wherever they take him, he chose to abstain from certain sensational effects that lay very close at hand in order to present a tenable case for a less self-seeking way of life, and in *The Duchess of Malfi* alternatives of a similar nature are held up for intensive scrutiny.[12] Man need not be a wolf to man, he may also be a god: expressed in extremely general terms this is the situation that the play illustrates and comments upon, and as a dramatic commentary it has few peers. Its depth, its "representational value," however, depends on how well the thematic aspects are related to the conflict that determines the course of the action, and we have noticed how strained the relationship often becomes, as minor incidents unexpectedly attract attention and divert interest from the issues at stake. It remains to see where the important emphases fall and thus determine the cumulative effect, the tragic impact, of *The Duchess of Malfi.*

This is naturally a question of themes, although not so much now their individual significance as their interdependence and common persuasiveness. Let us first consider a theme that seemed rather loosely connected with the central conflict of the play: the contrast between seeming and being, between appearance and reality. The key passage is again Bosola's taunting of the Old Lady and his subsequent meditation on the outward form of man, with its explicit reference to rottenness hidden in rich tissue. But the paradox is introduced much earlier. By the rapid revelation of the hideousness that is contained under the splendid surface of the Aragonian brothers the two are designated as the prime examples of this unpleasant aspect of society—of "painted honour," to use Bosola's words in a slightly altered sense. Soon their justice is also revealed as injustice, their piety as godlessness, and they themselves as "a kind of nothing." In the meantime their sister, who appeared false to the world, is proved true and even in death Duchess of Malfi. It is virtue, although not the "simple vertue" of decorum, that is hidden in her. Bosola, with his two natures occasionally referred to as garbs and symbolized by the masks he puts on, is obviously the character in whom the argument centers and who carries it to its logical conclusion. This is more than the standard reflections on the discrepancy between appearance and reality that intrigue and disguise plots usually call forth in the Elizabethan drama.[13] It is a deliberately created pattern, one that receives pronounced dramatic emphasis. It provides Webster with a frame of reference to which he can relate everything that happens in his tragedy, even that very essential thing, its basic conflict. It is a pervading though somewhat peripheral theme, which supports and adds perspective to other significantly elaborated ideas.

The central argument of *The Duchess of Malfi* is directly concerned with the issue that pits the Duchess and her husband against the Aragonian brothers, with both Bosola and the audience in judgment on the merits of each side's case. No matter how guilty Antonio and the Duchess may be—and the ambiguity of their position is never completely resolved—the attitude to be taken toward them is soon determined: as victims of cruel and unjustified persecution they are the natural center of sympathy in the play. By reducing their always severely limited power to none whatever, Webster concentrates on the universal aspect of their situation: they become every man, woman, and family subjected to the whim and violence of the forces of the world—not entirely but tolerably free from guilt. Being a woman and a great lady the Duchess is made to state the case for the defense: she can best represent not only their absolute helplessness but also their right to love, the natural right to "choose their Mates, And carroll their sweet pleasures to the Spring." The strident tones to which she first resorts serve to establish this "nature theme"; with a shrewd sense of the psychologically plausible Webster manages the crucial transfer from *actio* to *passio,* and toward the end *virtù* and integrity of life seem perfectly joined—innocence, nature, and fortitude married and murdered.[14]

Antonio is as powerless and should logically appear as innocent as his wife. So he does, but his innocence may be of a slightly different quality. His obvious virtue, remarkable passivity and tendency to moralize make up a combination that Webster has embodied on the stage before—in Cornelia and Marcello of *The White Devil.* The way in which Antonio "calls for his destruction" by visiting the Cardinal is the crowning example in Webster of the folly of innocence, the naïveté of the virtuous and weak. The sardonic note in the presentation is faint but should not be missed. Antonio is only technically the hero of *The Duchess of Malfi;* he is deliberately kept semianonymous till the end—not a prince but an attendant lord, or, more exactly, an obscure gentleman from Bologna, caught in the clutch of circumstance.

Although the Duchess is a prominent Elizabethan stage character in her own right, both she and Antonio are easily associated with abstract concepts and lend themselves well to a figurative reading of the play. The same is even more obviously true of the wicked Aragonian brothers, and the contrast between them and their victims in power and influence, moral outlook, and moral quality is maintained in a series of emblematic episodes, so that the general aspect of the conflict is emphasized until the significance of the Duchess' death has penetrated to Bosola and the audience. Yet the characters are no full-fledged abstractions. As acting parts they are necessarily shaped with some respect for psychological plausibility, and when the basic contrast between them need no longer be stressed, the presentation of the processes within their minds becomes a real concern with Webster. At the same time new themes are introduced. Retribution of the most ironically simplified kind overtakes Ferdinand, as an individual, to be sure, rather than as a representative of rampant violence. The Cardinal, hitherto supremely in control, shrinks and becomes an ordinary plotting villain, before he and his brother die in a veritable confusion of punishment, revenge and despair. For the theme of retribution is twisted and combined with that of futility, from whose frustrating effects nobody's plans are safe. As the end approaches, this aspect of life is developed and becomes the prevailing mood of the play, blatantly expressed in the echo scene and ironically illustrated in the maze of madness, conflicting purposes, and death that follows. When, at the close of *The Duchess of Malfi,* the theme of *integer vitae* is again sounded and its hopeful representative introduced, this dark mood cannot be dispelled. The amoral world is depicted as repellent in its rottenness, its safety and glory no more than illusions, and the moral alternative is stated unmistakably, firmly and as attractively as Webster's sense of realism permits, but even the moral individual will live in the general "shadow, or deepe pit of darknesse." And he may not live long.

This is the note on which *The Duchess of Malfi* ends. The captivating but seemingly capricious commentary on life that the play provides leads up to a point that is made with force and directness; Webster's is a consistent and cogent dramatic argument. Its tragic relevance dawns upon the audience slowly and painfully as the grotesque effects accumulate, but when, in the course of the final speeches, revelation comes of the full significance of what we have witnessed, the impact is extraordinary. There is no *White Devil* ambiguity about this ending. Everything appears to fall into place under the eyes of the spectator.

The effect, however, would have been recognizably less impressive if it had not been for the peculiar function and qualities of Bosola. After the Duchess' death he becomes the carrier of the "integrity theme," a transfer that is more plausible than it seems, since—without the audience realizing it fully—he has embodied the moral argument of the play from the very first. The thematic purpose of his divided allegiance is simple: principles of loyalty and the belly bind him to the world of the Aragonian brothers, principles of morality and the spirit to the world of the Duchess. In the service of pitiless power he may at times feel and express himself as an agent of necessity, with as little possibility to escape as his victims have, but throughout he remains able to repent and reform, although within the carefully observed limits of psychology and the imposed limits of the "futility theme." The tragedy of the Aragonian family, in which he takes such an active part, is performed for his benefit, in order to provide a valid answer to the argument in which his soul is involved. It is Bosola's dilemma, intimately connected with the probing into the problems of appearance as it is, that, expressed in words and action, gives the play its thematic unity.

It would nevertheless be an exaggeration to say that *The Duchess of Malfi* is Bosola's tragedy. As long as the Duchess is alive, she and Antonio occupy the center of interest; their importance to the argument is rapidly realized by the audience. In sanguine moments of assurance and self-dramatization we may hopefully identify ourselves with the Duchess, in more balanced and resigned moments we recognize Antonio behind our fears and doubts. But as the nature and implications of Bosola's moral conflict are understood, his dilemma, which originally seemed that of an inordinately repulsive cutthroat, becomes uncomfortably familiar. He is certainly the agent and not the victim of evil, but so may we easily become ourselves. As we listen to his rationalizations, we are watching the spirit of accommodation at work, in Bosola and in everybody. It is a disturbing and humiliating experience. Thus there are three characters in *The Duchess of Malfi* that should be taken to represent different reactions to the unhappy condition of man in an evil society: the well-meaning but passive Antonio, the energetic but impotent Duchess, and Bosola, the worm squirming on the hook where he has been induced to impale himself. Under such circumstances an unusually intricate interplay of related motives is unobtrusively brought about, and the consequences of the slightness of the basic story are definitely overcome. The immediacy and applicability of Webster's argument largely depend on his refusal to simplify vital issues. For every question that is answered in *The Duchess of Malfi,* a new one is raised. It is not only the importance but also the complexity of the problems that are pondered that makes the effect of the ending cut very deep. Our intellect is provoked, our emotions are engaged.

The presence in the play of a protagonist for good, however conglomerate, helps to make the issues clearer than in *The White Devil,* where such a figure is entirely lacking.[15] It also renders the world of the Duchess more acceptable as a representation of generally prevailing conditions than that of Vittoria, with its "existentialist" appreciation of action for its own sake. The differences between the two plays are, however, not fundamental. In *The Duchess of Malfi* we are still confronted with Webster's delicately balanced argument and preoccupation with the wearisome condition of humanity, which overshadows individual misfortunes and makes even the suffering and death of the Duchess an element only in a more comprehensive tragedy.

This is hardly surprising, for although the argument of *The Duchess of Malfi* is complete and self-sufficient, it is also a con-

tinuation of that of *The White Devil,* a reconsideration of the
same themes. Again Webster takes the power and attraction of
evil for granted, but no longer so dispassionately as before. In the
character of Antonio virtue may be presented as self-deceiving
and compromised, but never as dogmatic and almost ridiculous
in its unrealistic demands. In the character of the Duchess it has
become virtue in action, honorably adapted to the conditions of
life and influential by means of its example. The ground between
the extreme moral alternatives, which was left unexplored in *The
White Devil,* is now invaded by the Duchess, and the validity of
the experiment is belatedly recognized both by Bosola and the
audience. His conversion is an admission of the unique quality
of the virtuous life, to which there is no counterpart in *The
White Devil.*

But the admission, like the conversion, has a strictly limited
pertinence. It applies to a private and theoretical problem only,
and the pragmatic Webster is mainly interested in social and
practical effects. The conclusion of the play demonstrates, ironically but unmistakably, how restricted is the power of virtue and
how problematic the transformation of evil. It may occasionally
be defeated through self-destruction—as indicated by Ferdinand's
madness—but otherwise only through the workings of chance,
which rather than any force that might be called divine seems to
govern the world of the play.[16] We do not have judgment here.
Thus Webster arrives at the same conclusion as in *The White
Devil*—with greater reluctance and greater sadness because of the
glimpses of a better existence that have been gained, but also with
greater conviction.

The connections existing between Webster's tragedies and such
dramas as *The Malcontent, Women Beware Women,* and *The
Revenger's Tragedy,* in which the personal conflicts between
protagonists and antagonists also tend to disappear and major
characters are subordinated to a total effect of "tragic satire," have
been generally recognized. But an important distinction should

be made. Although *The Duchess of Malfi* and *The White Devil* are satiric and provoke disgust with many features of life, they also invite pity—in *The Duchess of Malfi* for both the individual sufferer and the general state of mankind. This connects the play closely with a Shakespearean tragedy to which, for equally specific purposes, I have compared *The White Devil:* namely *King Lear.* King, lord, beggar, and fool at the mercy of the powers of evil—in a dramatic situation that is caused by the same basic conflict Webster employed, Shakespeare too chose to resort to a "conglomerate protagonist" to bring home to the audience the full significance of the events. It would be unwise to claim that the questions raised by *The Duchess of Malfi* are of the same magnitude or expressed with the same vigor as in *King Lear,* a tragedy whose emotional impact will probably always remain unique. But Webster's play is, as I hope to have demonstrated, sufficiently relevant, complex, and impassioned to give us serious pause. By fair means and foul and with a richness of associations that befits the importance of his themes, he makes the spectator aware of the enormous span of human nature, within the soul and within society. The simple *exemplum,* provided by Bandello and his adapters, had served Webster well.

NOTES

I. The Story of the Duchess of Amalfi

1. For the historical background see F. Guicciardini, *Istoria d'Italia* (Milan, 1899), II, 13–112 (books V and VI); L. Simeoni, *Le Signorie* (Milan, 1950), pp. 761–766, and L. Volpicella, *Federico d'Aragona* (Naples, 1908).

2. For Lodovico d'Aragona see D. Morellini, *Giovanna d'Aragona duchessa d'Amalfi* (Cesena, 1906); L. v. Pastor, "Die Reise des Kardinals Luigi d'Aragona" in *Erläuterungen und Ergänzungen zu Janssens Geschichte des deutschen Volkes* (Freiburg i. B., 1905), vol. IV: 4, pp. 1–10; J. Webster, *The Duchess of Malfi* (ed. F. L. Lucas, Chatto & Windus, London, 1958), pp. 17–18. Permission to quote from this work has been kindly granted by editor and publisher. The work is subsequently quoted as Lucas. Cf. also L. Cardella, *Memorie storiche de' cardinali* (Rome, 1743), II, 274–275, and G. Moroni, *Dizionario di erudizione storicoecclesiastica* (Venice, 1840), II, 269–270. There is a short biography of him in MS Brancacciano IV. B. 1, f. 79, in Biblioteca Nazionale, Naples.

3. For Lodovico d'Aragona's relations with Julius II and Leo X see E. Rodocanachi, *Histoire de Rome. Le Pontificat de Jules II* (Paris, 1928), pp. 116–120; L. v. Pastor, *Geschichte der Päpste* (Freiburg i. B., 1901–1933), vols. III and IV, *passim* and esp. vol. III, pp. 791–792, 867, and vol. IV: 1, pp. 379, 389, 401; Pastor, "Die Reise des Kardinals Luigi d'Aragona," pp. 4–9. Cf. also contemporary reports such as P. de Grassi, *Le due spedizioni militari di Giulio II* (ed. L. Frati, Bologna, 1886), pp. 202, 222–226, 253–254, 289–290.

4. Pastor, *Geschichte der Päpste,* vol. IV: 1, p. 379. For the history of the Palazzo dei Penitenzieri see T. Magnuson, *Studies in Roman Quattrocento Architecture* (Stockholm, 1958), pp. 332–337.

5. The inscription runs:

D O M

Aloisio Car, Aragonio Regg, Neapolitann, Ferdinandi ne
poti Alefonsiq. prioris pronepoti, qvi vix, annos xliiii, m, iiii,
d, xv, Franciottus Car, Vrsinvs Ex, test, f, c, a, m d xxxiii,

ERGO CVNTA LICENT LACHESI TIBI NEC DATVR VLLI
EVITARE TVAS IMPROBA POSSE MANVS?
REGIBVS ILLE ATAVIS ALOISIVS AEDITVS, ILLE
CVI ROSEVS SACRO VERTICE FVLSIT APEX,
ILLE, VNI VIRTVS OMNIS CVI CONTIGIT, VNVS
QVI CONTRA HAEC POTVIT VIVERE, SAECLA TACET,
HEV QVOT NOS MORTALE GENVS SPERABIMVS ANNOS
SI VITA EST IPSIS TANTVLA NVMINIBVS?

The plaque is located exactly opposite the monument to Fra Angelico. The reclining statue above it is not of Lodovico d'Aragona but part of a monument to two cardinals of the Orsini family.

6. For the life of the Duchess see above all Morellini, *Giovanna d'Aragona,* esp. pp. 6–10. Cf. also M. Camera, *Memorie storico-diplomatiche dell' antica città e ducato di Amalfi* (Salerno, 1876–1881), II, 78–82, and Lucas, pp. 16–21.

7. There seems to be no real evidence that the Duchess and her children were murdered. Bandello and the Corona MSS are our only authorities, and it is notable that Filonico's *Vita della principessa di Francavilla* (MS X. C. 21, part VI, pp. 4–5, in Biblioteca Nazionale, Naples) reports that the victims were poisoned, not strangled. For the Duchess' flight from Amalfi see Notar Giacomo, *Cronica di Napoli* (ed. P. Garzilli, Naples, 1845), p. 331. Antonio is known to have died "ex vulneribus" in October 1513 (see Lucas, p. 21, note 1).

8. Cf. for instance Rodocanachi, *Histoire de Jules II,* pp. 116–120. But Bandello states that "uno dei gentiluomini andasse a Roma per le poste a trovar il cardinale." See M. Bandello, *Novelle* in *Raccolta di novellieri italiani* (Florence, 1833–1834), vol. I, p. 130, col. 1. This work is subsequently referred to as Bandello.

9. Bandello, pp. 127–131. With my discussion of Bandello cf. Lucas, pp. 19–21.

10. Cf. Morellini, *Giovanna d'Aragona,* pp. 20–22, as well as the same author's "La fonte di alcuni successi de' MSS Corona," *Napoli nobilissima,* XIV (Naples, 1905), pp. 77–79, 89–91. For a modern evaluation of Bandello's reliability see T. G. Griffith, *Bandello's Fiction. An Examination of the Novelle* (Oxford, 1955), pp. 1–22, 124–138.

11. See Morellini, *Giovanna d'Aragona,* pp. 18–20, and Lucas, p. 21.

12. This attempt at establishing a chronology is based on information in Pastor, *Geschichte der Päpste,* III, 854–858; Simeoni, *Le signorie,* pp. 804–805, 811–812, 973, and J. Dierauer, *Geschichte der schweizerischen Eidgenossenschaft* (Gotha, 1920–1924), II, 494–518. Cf. Guicciardini, *Istoria d'Italia,* III, 27–64 (parts of books X and XI).

13. Cf. however P. Rébora, *L'Italia nel dramma inglese* (Milan, 1925), pp. 201–202.

14. Bandello, p. 129, col. 1.

15. Bandello does not say which brother it is who knows how to "menar le mani."

16. Bandello, p. 131, col. 2.

17. *Ibid.,* pp. 127, col. 2; 128, col. 1.

18. *Ibid.,* p. 128, col. 1.

19. *Ibid.,* p. 128, col. 1.

20. The MSS I have consulted are I. D. 37, ff. 43–48; I. D. 38, pp. 40–47; I. D. 39, ff. 66v–76r; X. A. 33, ff. 42v–47r; X. B. 67, ff. 7v–8v; X. C. 15, ff. 47–53; X. C. 21, part I, pp. 111–112; part II, ff. 60v–70v; part VI, pp. 4–5; X. C. 32, ff. 2–16; X. C. 34, ff. 19v–23r; XIII. AA. 13, ff. 29v–34r; Brancacciano III. B. 9, pp. 80–91; San Martino 64, ff. 71v–79v, 135–143, all in Biblioteca Nazionale, Naples (cf. Morellini, "La fonte di alcuni successi de' MSS Corona"). There are also two versions preserved in Biblioteca Nazionale Braidense, Milan: MSS A. C. 10, ff. 80–95, and A. D. XIV. 36, pp. 29–36. My quotations are from MSS X. C. 21 and X. B. 67.

21. MS. X. C. 21, part I, f. 64r. The italics are mine.

22. MS X. B. 67, ff. 7v–8v. Cf. f. 239r.

23. MS X. B. 67, f. 8v.

24. The editions used are F. de Belleforest, *Histoires tragiques* (Paris, 1565), where the Duchess' story is number nineteen and occurs in vol. II, ff. 1–30, and W. Painter, *The Palace of Pleasure* (ed. J. Jacobs, London, 1890), where it is number twenty-three (tome II) and occurs in vol. III, pp. 3–43. These works are subsequently referred to as Belleforest and Painter. For an analysis of Belleforest's art of translating see F. Hook, *The French Bandello,* The University of Missouri Studies, XXII (Columbia, 1948), pp. 9–20. The Elizabethan editions of Painter show no significant variations.

25. Lucas, pp. 22–23. Cf. K. Kiesow, "Die verschiedenen Bearbeitungen der Novelle von der Herzogin von Amalfi des Bandello in den Literaturen des XVI und XVII Jahrhunderts," *Anglia,* XVII (Halle, 1895): 208–209.

26. Painter, III, 40; Belleforest, vol. II, f. 28v.

27. Painter, III, 42; Belleforest, vol. II, f. 30r.

28. Painter, III, 25; Belleforest, vol. II, f. 17r.

29. Painter, III, 37; Belleforest, vol. II, f. 26r.

30. Painter, III, 32–33; Belleforest, vol. II, ff. 22r–23r.

31. Painter, III, 42; Belleforest, vol. II, f. 30r.

32. Painter, III, 32–33; Belleforest, vol. II, f. 22.

33. Painter, III, 9; Belleforest, vol. II, f. 5v.

34. Painter, III, 11; Belleforest, vol. II, f. 5r (so numbered, but really f. 7r). Elsewhere in the "nouel" Antonio's behavior is said to resemble that of "the Mad and Bedlem persons which haue before their eyes, the figured Fansies whych cause the conceipt of their fury." See Painter, III, 12; Belleforest, vol. II, f. 7v, and cf. M. C. Bradbrook, *Themes and Conventions of Elizabethan Tragedy* (Cambridge, 1935), p. 198.

35. Painter, III, 34; Belleforest, vol. II, f. 24r.

36. Painter, III, 40; Belleforest, vol. II, f. 28v; Bandello, p. 131, col. 2.

37. Painter, III, 27; Belleforest, vol. II, f. 19r.

38. Painter, III, 24; Belleforest, vol. II, f. 16v.

39. Painter, III, 8, 9; Belleforest, vol. II, f. 7r (so numbered, but really f. 5r).

40. Painter, III, 14; Belleforest, vol. II, f. 9r.

41. Painter, III, 18; Belleforest, vol. II, f. 12r.

42. Painter, III, 8; Belleforest, vol. II, f. 6v (so numbered, but really f. 4v).

43. Painter, III, 13; Belleforest, vol. II, f. 8v.

44. Painter, III, 36; Belleforest, vol. II, f. 25r.

45. Painter, III, 36; Belleforest, vol. II, f. 25v. The death of the children is also made much of by Belleforest–Painter, who describe them as falling "vpon their knees before those Tyrants, and embracinge their Legges" (Painter, III, 37; Belleforest, vol. II, f. 26r).

46. Painter, III, 36; Belleforest, vol. II, f. 25v.

47. H. C., *The Forrest of Fancy* (London, 1579), sig. N 1v–N 2r; R. Greene, *Gwydonius; the Carde of Fancie* (London, 1584), sig. M 1r.

48. Greene, *The Carde of Fancie,* sig. M 1r.

49. G. Whetstone, *An Heptameron of Ciuill Discourses* (London, 1582), sig. Q 2v.

50. T. Beard, *The Theatre of Gods Judgements* (London, 1597), pp. 321–323.

51. *Ibid.,* p. 323.

52. S. Goulart, *Admirable and Memorable Histories* (transl. E. Grimeston, London, 1607), pp. 364–367, where the story of the Duchess appears under the heading "Secret and vnequall marriages vnfortunate."

53. *Ibid.,* p. 367.

54. *Ibid.,* p. 364.

55. *Ibid.,* p. 367.

56. See D. T. Starnes, "Barnabe Riche's 'Sappho Duke of Mantona,' " *Studies in Philology,* XXX (1933): 455–472, and T. M. Cranfill, "Barnabe Riche's 'Sappho' and *The Weakest Goeth to the Wall,*" University of Texas Studies in English 1945–1946 (Austin, 1946), pp. 166–177. See also B. Riche, *Rich's Farewell to Military Profession* (ed. T. M. Cranfill, Austin, 1959), pp. xxxviii–xxxix, 339–340. This is the edition subsequently referred to.

57. *Rich's Farewell,* pp. 36–37.

58. *Ibid.,* p. 61.

59. *Ibid.,* p. 62.

60. The text used is in Lope de Vega, *Obras* (Madrid, 1913–1930), XV, 191–231. For earlier comments on the relationship between Lope's play and Webster's *Duchess of Malfi* see Kiesow, "Die verschiedenen Bearbeitungen,"

pp. 254–257; Morellini, *Giovanna d'Aragona,* pp. 91–93, and Lucas, pp. 23–25. For the Cinthio–Lope connection see A. Gasparetti, "Giovanni Battista Giraldi e Lope de Vega," *Annales de la faculté des lettres de Bordeaux et des universités du Midi. Bulletin hispanique,* XXXII (1930): 372–403.

61. Lope de Vega, *Obras,* vol. XV, p. 223, col. 1.

II. Potential Secondary Sources

1. For a pioneer study of this aspect see C. Crawford, "John Webster and Sir Philip Sidney," *Notes and Queries,* 10th Series, II (1904): 221–223, 261–263, 303–304, 342–343, 381–382, and for the most modern treatment the continuous commentary in R. W. Dent, *John Webster's Borrowing* (Berkeley and Los Angeles, 1960), pp. 174–265, subsequently referred to as Dent. The text of *Arcadia* used here is in P. Sidney, *The Complete Works* (ed. A. Feuillerat, Cambridge, 1922–1926), subsequently referred to as Sidney.

2. Sidney, II, 161.

3. *Ibid.,* I, 332.

4. *Ibid.,* I, 333.

5. *Ibid.,* I, 470.

6. *Ibid.,* I, 492.

7. *Ibid.,* I, 352–353.

8. *Old Fortunatus,* I, i, 1–63, in T. Dekker, *The Dramatic Works* (ed. F. T. Bowers, Cambridge, 1953–1962), I, 116–118.

9. *II The Return from Parnassus,* II, ii, in *The Three Parnassus Plays* (ed. J. B. Leishman, London, 1949), pp. 263–265.

10. *Cynthia's Revels,* I, ii; I, iii, 1–11, in B. Jonson, *Works* (ed. C. H. Herford and P. Simpson, Oxford, 1925–1950), IV, 48–52; T. Lodge, *The Wounds of Civil War,* III, i, 1219–1244, Malone Society Reprints (Oxford, 1910); R. Tailor, *The Hog hath Lost his Pearl,* IV, i, in *A Select Collection of Old English Plays* (ed. R. Dodsley and W. C. Hazlitt, London, 1874–1876), XI, 477–478. For other echo scenes see Lucas, pp. 203–204.

11. Sidney, I, 353.

12. *The Times Library Supplement,* June 18, 1954. Dent, p. 229, rejects Praz's theory, but without noticing the support it receives from the proximity of the two stories in Bandello.

13. Herodotus, *The Famous Hystory* (transl. B. R., London, 1584), ff. 101r–103r; Bandello, pp. 122–126.

14. Bandello, p. 126, col. 2. Herodotus, *The Famous Hystory,* f. 103r, has a slightly different emphasis: "The Lady that had listned to his tale, hearing the newes she longed for, stretched out her hand to lay hold on him, who subtilly presenting her with the hande of his brother, (which beeing darke, she fast griped in stead of his owne) hee conveyed himselfe from her and was no more seene."

15. Bandello, p. 126, col. 2; Herodotus, *The Famous Hystory*, f. 103r.

16. See Gasparetti, "Giovanni Battista Giraldi," pp. 372–403. The text used here is *Gli ecatommiti del Giraldi* in *Raccolta di novellieri italiani*, II, 1859–1866, subsequently referred to as Cinthio. The French translation by G. Chappuys, *Cent excellentes nouvelles de M. Jean Baptiste Giraldy Cynthien, gentilhomme ferrarois* (Paris, 1583–1584), vol. I, ff. 193–206, is very faithful to the original.

17. Cinthio, p. 1860, col. 1.

18. *Ibid.*, p. 1860, col. 2.

19. *Ibid.*, p. 1861, col. 1.

20. *Ibid.*, p. 1859, col. 2.

21. *Ibid.*, p. 1860, col. 1.

22. *Ibid.*, p. 1863, col. 1.

23. *Ibid.*, p. 1863, col. 2.

24. Goulart, *Admirable and Memorable Histories*, pp. 386–387. See also Lucas, pp. 198–199, and cf. M. C. Bradbrook, "Two Notes upon Webster," *Modern Language Review*, XLII (1947): 284.

25. See Dent, pp. 179, 187, 206–207, 231, 262–263.

26. Goulart, *Admirable and Memorable Histories*, pp. 37, 519. According to Guicciardini Ferdinand d'Avalos, Marquis of "Pisquairo," was neither old, nor very honorable: "though he had not past the age of xxxvi. yeres, yet for experience he was olde, for inuencion suttle, in councell grave, in execution resolute, wise to forsee a daunger, and quicke to avoid a mischiefe . . . prowd of minde, of wit deceitfull, of nature malicious, of councell and action without sincerity . . . in all Italy there was not a more impious and disloyall man." *The Historie of Guicciardin* (transl. G. Fenton, London, 1579), p. 944; *Istoria d'Italia*, III, 385.

27. *The Historie of Guicciardin*, p. 903; *Istoria d'Italia*, III, 340.

28. *The Historie of Guicciardin*, pp. 578, 583; *Istoria d'Italia*, II, 381, 387. It should perhaps also be mentioned that reference is repeatedly made to "Malatesta Baillon" and "Federicke Bossolo" and once to the latter's supervision of the murder of "Gentill Baillon" (*The Historie of Guicciardin*, p. 1076; *Istoria d'Italia*, IV, 126).

29. See *The Historie of Guicciardin*, p. 650; *Istoria d'Italia*, III, 59–60.

30. Lucas, pp. 26–27. According to T. Bogard, *The Tragic Satire of John Webster* (Berkeley and Los Angeles, 1955), pp. 17–19, Webster's interest in contemporary events was conspicuous, and paralleled only by Chapman's.

31. See for instance R. Brooke, *John Webster and the Elizabethan Drama* (London, 1917), pp. 241–243, and Lucas, pp. 14–15:

32. This theory has been questioned by J. R. Brown, "On the Dating of Webster's *The White Devil* and *The Duchess of Malfi*," *Philological Quarterly*, XXXI (1952): 353–362, but is still upheld by Lucas, p. 15, note 2. See also C. Leech, "An Addendum on Webster's Duchess," *PQ*, XXXVII

(1958): 254–255, and, for the close resemblance to Chapman's Biron plays, Miss Bradbrook, "Two Notes upon Webster," pp. 292–293.

33. *Relation exacte de tout ce qui s'est passé à la mort du maréchal d'Ancre*, quoted in A. Franklin, *La cour de France et l'assassinat du maréchal d'Ancre* (Paris, 1914), p. 281.

34. Among many examples the following might be mentioned: *II The Honest Whore*, IV, i, 34–42, in T. Dekker, *The Dramatic Works* (ed. Bowers), II, 182; *The Four Prentices of London*, I, i, in T. Heywood, *Dramatic Works* (London, 1874), II, 192; *Every Man out of his Humour*, II, iii, 18–23, in B. Jonson, *Works* (ed. Herford and Simpson), III, 469–470; *Eastward Ho*, II, ii, 332–335, 354–357; IV, ii, 217, in B. Jonson, *Works*, IV, 552–553, 593; *The Malcontent*, Induction, in J. Marston, *The Plays* (ed. H. H. Wood, Edinburgh and London, 1934), I, 142, and Hamlet's familiar exchange with Osric in V, ii.

35. *Monsieur d'Olive*, II, ii, 28–35, in G. Chapman, *The Plays and Poems of George Chapman: The Comedies* (ed. T. M. Parrott, London, 1914), p. 326.

36. F. Beaumont and J. Fletcher, *The Works* (ed. A. Glover and A. R. Waller, Cambridge, 1905–1912), VIII, 205; *Love's Labour's Lost*, V, i, 92–94, in The Arden Shakespeare (ed. R. David, London, 1960), pp. 127–128, and note to line 93.

37. M. de Montaigne, *Essays* (transl. J. Florio, ed. J. I. M. Stewart, London, 1931), I, 303. The parallel has been overlooked by both Dent and R. F. Whitman, *The Opinion of Wisdom: Montaigne and John Webster*, unpublished dissertation (Harvard College Library, 1956). Cf. also Whitman's "Webster's *Duchess of Malfi*," *N&Q*, new series, VI (1959): 174–175.

Antonio's reference to the great reverence shown to the sovereign at the English court agrees with other sources of information. Only very rarely was anyone allowed to remain covered in the royal presence. The following instance might be adduced from G. Cavendish, *The Life and Death of Cardinal Wolsey* (ed. R. S. Sylvester, Early English Text Society, London, 1959), p. 94: "[Wolsey] whome the Kyng receyved wt as amyable a chere as euer he dyd & called hyme a side and led hyme by the hand to a great wyndowe where he talked wt hyme And caused hyme to be Couered." L. Hotson, *The First Night of* Twelfth Night (London, 1954), pp. 202, 230, quotes Virginio Orsini's words to the effect that he was allowed to be covered in Queen Elizabeth's presence, obviously since he enjoyed the same age-old privilege of the grandees at the Spanish court (p. 218).

38. For Webster's use of such material see Dent's Commentary, where many hitherto unnoticed instances of verbal echoes are listed.

39. For an evaluation of the influence of Montaigne on Webster, Whitman, *The Opinion of Wisdom*, is useful but unfortunately unavailable to the great majority of scholars. Mario Praz comments at some length on the relationship in *Tre drammi elisabettiani* (Naples, 1958), pp. 206–209.

III. Analysis of the Documents

1. See J. Webster, *The White Devil and The Duchess of Malfy* (ed. M. W. Sampson), The Belles-lettres Series, III: 3 (Boston and London, 1904), pp. xxxvii–xxxviii.

2. Sidney, I, 24, 208, 485. The corresponding passages in *D.M.* are V, ii, 314–315; IV, ii, 391–392; IV, i, 108–111.

3. Painter, III, 38, 13; *D.M.*, II, v, 87–91; IV, ii, 29–30. The latter quotation is a commonplace, ultimately derived from Seneca (see Dent, p. 235), but its occurrence in Painter should be noted.

4. Painter, III, 12, 26; *D.M.*, I, i, 507–508; IV, ii, 22–25.

5. Cf. the passages with *D.M.*, II, v and IV, ii, 248–268.

6. The Cardinal suggests that Bosola should hire a dozen *bravi* to kill Antonio (Goulart, *Admirable and Memorable Histories*, p. 379). Cf. *D.M.*, V, ii, 346–347.

7. Bandello, p. 129, col. 1; Painter, III, 20.

8. Bandello, p. 127, col. 1; Lucas, p. 165.

9. Bandello's thirty-second novella is dedicated "all' illustrissimo e reverendissimo signore Lodovico d'Aragona cardinale" (Bandello, p. 156).

10. The pertinent passages in the plays are Lope de Vega, *Obras*, XV, 197, and *D.M.*, II, i, 121–134.

11. See Chapter II (references in notes 24 and 25).

12. Lucas, p. 23. Cf. Kiesow, "Die verschiedenen Bearbeitungen," pp. 240–244.

13. Painter, III, 42; Belleforest, vol. II, f. 30r.

14. Painter, III, 20. Belleforest, vol. II, f. 13v, is more exact.

15. Painter, III, 36; Belleforest, vol. II, f. 25r.

16. Sidney, I, 470, and cf. Chapter I, note 35.

17. According to Mario Praz, "John Webster and *The Maid's Tragedy*," *English Studies*, XXXVII (1956): 258, "the episode in *The Second Maiden's Tragedy* of the corpse dressed as by a modern mortician, which owes much to the episode of Hermione's statue in *The Winter's Tale*, may have combined with this latter and with the reminiscence of the mock corpses in *Arcadia* III to suggest the wax figures in *The Duchess of Malfi*."

18. See Chapter I.

19. Painter's dating of the main events leaves nothing to be desired. Antonio is said to have accompanied King Frederick of Aragon to France and the Duchess' tragedy to have taken place "almost in our tyme, when the French vnder leadinge of that notable Capitayne Gaston de Foix, vanquished the force of Spayne and Naples at the Iourney of Ravenna in the time of the French Kynge called Lewes the twelfth, who married the Lady Mary, Daughter to Kynge Henry the seuenth, and Sister to the Victorious Prynce of worthy memory kynge Henry the eyght" (Painter, III, 4; Belleforest, vol. II, f. 2, is less explicit). That the battle was fought

and the Duchess killed while Julius II was Pope is also made clear by
Painter, whose only mistake is to place the murder of Antonio within the
reign of the same Pope (Painter, p. 42; Belleforest, f. 30r). Webster's dating
of the horoscope shows that he was aware in which period the events were
supposed to have taken place.

20. Cinthio, p. 1861, col. 2.

21. The parallel between the Duchess' momentary return to life and
Desdemona's (*Othello*, V, ii, 118–126) does not affect our conclusion. Cf.
Lucas, p. 197, and the Arden *Othello* (ed. M. R. Ridley, London, 1958),
pp. 182–184, esp. note to line 118.

22. It should be noted that F. M. Todd, "Webster and Cervantes,"
MLR, LI (1956): 321–323, makes a case for another interpolation at about
the same time and considers *D.M.*, V, v, 95–98, derived from *Don Quixote*,
either in the Spanish edition of 1615 or the French translation of 1618.
Dent's reasons (p. 264) for rejecting this theory seem adequate.

23. For the purpose of this study it would be wrong to consider the
short discussion of the Duchess of Amalfi in Whetstone's *Heptameron* a
source of Webster's.

IV. The Nature of the Material

1. Cf. my *Sources of* The White Devil (Uppsala, 1957), pp. 140–144.

2. For different interpretations of such episodes in the Elizabethan drama
see L. B. Wright, "Madmen as Vaudeville Performers on the Elizabethan
Stage," *Journal of English and Germanic Phililogy*, XXX (1931): 48–54;
J. T. McCullen, Jr., "Madness and the Isolation of Characters in Elizabethan and Early Stuart Drama," *SP*, XLVIII (1951): 206–218, and above
all R. R. Reed, Jr., *Bedlam on the Jacobean Stage* (Cambridge, Mass.,
1952), pp. 40–64, esp. pp. 44–47 (on *The Duchess of Malfi*). Cf. also S. I.
Hayakawa, "A Note on the Madmen's Scene in Webster's *The Duchess of
Malfi*," *Publications of the Modern Language Association of America*,
XLVII (1932): 907–909, and C. W. Davies, "The Structure of *The Duchess
of Malfi*," *English*, XII (1958), pp. 89–93.

3. Dent is now the authority on this aspect of Webster's art.

4. For Webster's debt to J. Bignon, *A Briefe, But An Effectuall Treatise
of the Election of Popes* (London, 1605), see J. R. Brown, "The Papal
Election in John Webster's 'The White Devil' (1612)," *N&Q*, new series,
IV (1957): 490–494, and cf. Dent, pp. 130–133.

5. See *The Sources of* The White Devil, pp. 133–135.

6. For one of the best evaluations of Belleforest's moral attitude see
Webster, *The White Devil and The Duchess of Malfy* (ed. Sampson), pp.
xxxvi–xxxviii. Miss Bradbrook's reading of the "nouel" (*Themes and
Conventions*, pp. 198–199) is equally understanding, whereas Lucas, p. 22,
Bogard, *Tragic Satire*, p. 17, note 9, and F. W. Wadsworth, "Webster's

Duchess of Malfi in the Light of Some Contemporary Ideas on Marriage and Remarriage," *PQ*, XXXV (1956), pp. 399–401, stress Belleforest's intolerance and lack of subtlety.

7. Cf. F. T. Bowers, *Elizabethan Revenge Tragedy 1587–1642* (Gloucester, Mass., 1959), pp. 64–65, 94.

8. For discussions of the Elizabethan background to the Duchess' case see Miss Bradbrook, *Themes and Conventions*, pp. 198–201; C. Leech, *John Webster* (London, 1951), pp. 69–72, and above all Wadsworth, "Webster's *Duchess of Malfi*," pp. 396–402.

9. Whetstone, *Heptameron*, sig. Q 2v.

10. Dent, pp. 3–56, presents a detailed and convincing case for "Webster's imitation," based exclusively on the great number of more or less easily recognizable echoes from other writers that his plays contain. Cf. also *The White Devil* (ed. J. R. Brown), The Revels Plays (London, 1960), pp. xxxv–xxxviii.

V. A CLARIFICATION OF ISSUES

1. Lucas, p. 31.

2. For this aspect of Webster's art see Bogard, *Tragic Satire*, esp. pp. 117–145, and A. Kernan, *The Cankered Muse* (New Haven, 1959), pp. 232–246.

3. For a final verdict on the by-plot see Chapter VI.

4. See H. T. Price, "The Function of Imagery in Webster," *PMLA*, LXX (1955): 717–739, and I. Glier, *Struktur und Gestaltungsprinzipien in den Dramen John Websters* (Munich, 1957), pp. 150–159. Cf. also W. Clemen, *Schein und Sein bei Shakespeare* (Munich, 1959).

5. Cf. Whitman, *The Opinion of Wisdom*, pp. 101–103.

6. For favorable comments on Bosola's "meditation" see Bogard, *Tragic Satire*, pp. 132–133, and Kernan, *The Cankered Muse*, pp. 234–236, while W. A. Edwards, "John Webster," *Determinations* (ed. F. R. Leavis) (London, 1934), pp. 161–164, considers the baiting of the Old Lady a mere excrescency.

7. But cf. Dent, pp. 26–37.

8. The debate on this issue continues. To Kiesow's and Stoll's familiar condemnations of the Duchess (Kiesow, "Die verschiedenen Bearbeitungen," p. 251, and E. E. Stoll, *John Webster*, Boston, 1905, pp. 130, 192) have been added the more temperate observations of Davies, "The Structure of *The Duchess of Malfi*," pp. 92–93, and McD. Emslie, "Motives in Malfi. The F. L. Lucas Edition of Webster," *Essays in Criticism*, IX (1959), pp. 396, 400. Among the Duchess' defenders Mr. Lucas is still prominent (see his note on p. 35) and his opinion is supported by Wadsworth, "Webster's *Duchess of Malfi*," pp. 400–401, 407. The efforts of Miss Bradbrook, *Themes and Conventions*, pp. 198–209, and Leech, *John Webster*, pp. 68–81, to present both sides of the argument have created some critical

confusion. Cf. Leech, "An Addendum on Webster's Duchess," pp. 253–256.

9. R. Ornstein, *The Moral Vision of Jacobean Tragedy* (Madison, 1960), p. 141, comments in a similar vein: "Her marriage to a man unworthy of her is a disastrous mistake, yet one she never regrets and which she redeems by the beauty and selflessness of her devotion. Moreover, it is not the marriage itself which is shameful but the moral compromise involved in hiding it."

10. Cf. Leech, *John Webster*, pp. 78–79. It might also be pointed out that the only official suitor Webster furnishes the Duchess with is the impossible Malateste—a striking addition to the original story.

11. The Duchess' "Thou art a superstitious fool" in answer to Cariola's warning "I do not like this jesting with religion, This faigned Pilgrimage" (III, ii, 365–368) strikes a more impatient note. For this "falsification of religion" see Davies, "The Structure of *The Duchess of Malfi*," pp. 92–93, and cf. Leech, *John Webster*, pp. 75–76, and P. Haworth, *English Hymns and Ballads* (Oxford, 1927), pp. 102–103.

12. Painter, III, 9; Belleforest, vol. II, f. 5v.

13. Wadsworth, "Webster's *Duchess of Malfi*," pp. 405–407, takes a more favorable view of Antonio, who is regarded as "an ideally acceptable husband," while the opposite opinion is maintained by Ornstein, *The Moral Vision*, pp. 142–145, who considers him more contemptible than Bosola.

14. The "spirit of woman" has been interpreted in different ways—as fear by Bogard, *Tragic Satire*, pp. 65–66, as womanly instincts by Haworth, *English Hymns and Ballads*, pp. 100–101, and as sacred and profane love by Ornstein, *The Moral Vision*, p. 148.

15. Painter, III, 33; Belleforest, vol. II, ff. 22v–23r.

16. For comments on the relationship between the Duchess and Ferdinand see Lucas, pp. 33–34; Leech, *John Webster*, pp. 99–105, and G. Baldini, *John Webster e il linguaggio della tragedia* (Rome, 1953), pp. 154–155.

17. Cf. Lucas, p. 33, and Bogard, *Tragic Satire*, pp. 53–54.

18. Cf. I. Jack, "The Case of John Webster," *Scrutiny*, XVI (1949): 42, and Emslie, "Motives in Malfi," p. 392.

19. Kernan, *The Cankered Muse*, pp. 233–242, and Ornstein, *The Moral Vision*, pp. 142–148, make valuable contributions to the understanding of Bosola's character. See also C. G. Thayer, "The Ambiguity of Bosola," *SP*, LIV (1957): 162–171.

20. Cf. Ornstein, *The Moral Vision*, pp. 143–144, where Bosola is characterized as "the feudal liege brought up to Jacobean date."

21. Cf. Thayer, "The Ambiguity of Bosola," p. 165.

VI. THE ISSUES RESOLVED

1. And ('cause she'll needes be mad) I am resolv'd

To remove forth the common Hospitall
All the mad-folke, and place them neere her lodging.

(IV, i, 151–153)

For the madmen's scene see the references given above, Chapter IV, note 2.

2. For a provocative study of Act IV along "ritualistic" lines see I. S. Ekeblad, "The 'Impure Art' of John Webster," *Review of English Studies,* IX (1958): 253–267, where the author argues persuasively in favor of an intended charivari effect. Since "even the marriage-festival of the Princess Elizabeth was cheered with a masque of lunatics" (Lucas, p. 189), such an interpretation is, however, very dangerous. It was in fact Campion's *The Lord's Maske* with its dance of "twelve franticks . . . all represented in sundry habits and humours" that was performed. See J. Nicolls, *Progresses, Processions, and Magnificent Festivities of King James the First* (London, 1828), II, 554–555, and T. Campion, *Works* (ed. A. H. Bullen, London, 1889), p. 194.

3. For a fuller discussion of Webster's horror devices see Chapter VII.

4. Cf. for instance Miss Bradbrook, *Themes and Conventions,* p. 197. The Hieronymus Bosch-like precision of Webster's description of strange torments has been commented upon by Baldini, *John Webster,* p. 159, note 1 (actually a minor appendix). Cf. also F. Olivero, *Studi britannici* (Turin, 1931), p. 52.

5. *The Devil's Law-Case,* IV, ii, 277, in J. Webster, *The Complete Works* (ed. F. L. Lucas, London, 1927), vol. II.

6. Cf. also Bosola's reference to the "Larke in a cage" (IV, ii, 127–131).

7. Lucas, p. 34. This opinion is shared by Haworth, *English Hymns and Ballads,* p. 75, and to a certain extent by Leech, *John Webster,* pp. 65–66, while Thayer, "The Ambiguity of Bosola," pp. 162–163, and Lord David Cecil, *Poets and Story-Tellers* (London, 1949), p. 39, insist on the great relevance and impact of the fifth act.

8. Cf. Whitman, *The Opinion of Wisdom,* pp. 104–106.

9. *The White Devil,* V, vi, 273–274, in *The Complete Works,* vol. I. For a fuller discussion see *The Sources of* The White Devil, pp. 158–180.

10. *The White Devil,* V, vi, 256–258.

11. See *The Sources of* The White Devil, p. 175, and cf. Leech, *John Webster,* p. 89. But cf. also Bogard, *Tragic Satire,* pp. 38–44, and Whitman, *The Opinion of Wisdom,* pp. 164–166.

12. It is important to realize the limited significance of the final "victory of virtue" in Webster—the only background against which such statements as "always at the end of Webster's plays the Divine Law is vindicated" (Cecil, *Poets and Story-Tellers,* p. 34) can be accepted.

VII. A JACOBEAN TRAGEDY

1. Reed, *Bedlam on the Jacobean Stage,* pp. 85–88, considers Webster's delineation of Ferdinand "a study not unworthy of Shakespeare."

2. The exceptions are few, the most obvious one occurring in V, iv, 27–34, which comes close to the *locus classicus* in *The White Devil*—II, i, 386–389.

3. For an analysis of the malcontent element in Bosola see Kernan, *The Cankered Muse*, pp. 233–242.

4. This is the most obviously conventional contradiction in Webster's characterization. As the major-domo is certainly not supposed to be a brilliant conversationalist once his description of the major characters is over, the flippant tone which is struck in order to make his comments more telling becomes somewhat confusing.

5. For the meaning of the horoscope see J. Parr, "The Horoscope in Webster's *The Duchess of Malfi*," *PMLA*, LX (1945): 760–765.

6. For unfavorable verdicts on this aspect of Webster's plays see Edwards, "John Webster," pp. 170–171, and Jack, "The Case of John Webster," p. 43.

7. Baldini, *John Webster*, p. 169.

8. Cf. Jack, "The Case of John Webster," p. 43.

9. But cf. Leech, *John Webster*, p. 75.

10. Cf. Edwards, "John Webster," p. 164.

11. See Baldini, *John Webster*, pp. 153–156.

12. See *The Sources of* The White Devil, pp. 161–168.

13. Cf., in addition to Chapter V, Clemen, *Schein und Sein bei Shakespeare*, pp. 6–11.

14. Kernan's verdict on the Duchess is worth remembering; she is not only "a nobly born woman, but, as language and scenes reveal, the very spirit of love, life, joy and society" (*The Cankered Muse*, p. 240).

15. See *The Sources of* The White Devil, p. 184.

16. Whitman, *The Opinion of Wisdom*, pp. 184–192, considers Webster's religion that of a skeptic; Cecil, *Poets and Story-Tellers*, pp. 29–31, finds it thoroughly Calvinistic—to mention the extreme interpretations.

INDEX